"SLAPPING US RIGHT IN THE FACE WITH THEIR MESSAGE."

Tom Taxena, hired producer, Cadillac Flash Eagles

An AVA Book
Published by AVA Publishing SA
c/o Fidinter SA
Ch. de la Joliette 2
Case postale 96
1000 Lausanne 6
Switzerland
Tel: +41 786 005 109
Email: enquiries@avabooks.ch

Distributed by Thames and Hudson (ex-North America)
181a High Holborn
London WC1V 7QX
United Kingdom
Tel: +44 20 7845 5000
Fax: +44 20 7845 5055
Email: sales@thameshudson.co.uk
www.thamesandhudson.com

Distributed by Sterling Publishing Co., Inc.
in the USA
387 Park Avenue South
New York, NY 10016-8810
Tel: +1 212 532 7160
Fax: +1 212 213 2495
www.sterlingpub.com

in Canada
Sterling Publishing
c/o Canadian Manda Group
One Atlantic Avenue, Suite 105
Toronto, Ontario M6K 3E7

English Language Support Office
AVA Publishing (UK) Ltd.
Tel: +44 1903 204 455
Email: enquiries@avabooks.co.uk

ISBN 2-88479-036-5

10 9 8 7 6 5 4 3 2 1

Series design concept by HSAG Design Ltd.
Layout by Mark Roberts

Production and separations by AVA Book Production
Pte. Ltd., Singapore
Tel: +65 6334 8173
Fax: +65 6334 0752
Email: production@avabooks.com.sg

AVA Publishing SA
Switzerland

MARKETING YOUR CREATIVITY

New Approaches for a Changing Industry

MATT PERRY & ANT MELDER

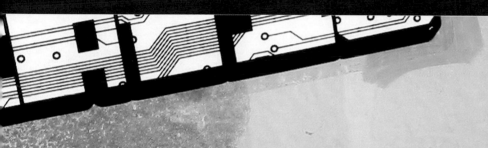

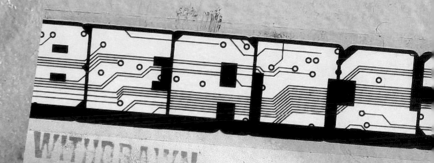

CONTENTS

00 INTRODUCTION

IN THE FUTURE, THERE WON'T BE SUCH A THING AS A CREATIVE DEPARTMENT. IF THERE IS, IT WILL BE MUCH SMALLER.

Finding the right role for you in a changing creative landscape

You've just come through college with flying colours. Breezed an A in your Graphic Design diploma, sailed through your Advertising course, passed your Digital Design degree without breaking into a sweat. Your course-topping portfolio's brimming with bright ideas, your design skills are sharp and your confidence is high. What's your next step? Dig out the Yellow Pages, call up London's most famous ad agency and ask to speak to Mr Saatchi, right? Wrong. Hang fire.

You're a junior creative at a modest agency. You've just worked your fifth late night in a row, you're shipwrecked on trade ads, feel your talent wasting slowly away and you're sick of the taste of instant coffee and cheap pizza. What now? Dig out your CV, get ready to put on your best telephone voice and call up that recruitment consultant, right? Not necessarily.

the party holds

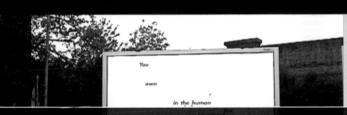

Figure 0.1
Billboard story by Toby Bradbury.

You're a creative at an agency with a decent name around town. The shelves are bulging with awards and the MD appears in Campaign and Creative Review on a regular basis. Everything seemed to be going well. Two years ago. Problem is, nothing's changed since then. Same wages, same briefs, same account execs coming back from client presentations with the same excuses for not selling the concepts you worked the same long hours on. Nothing new is going into your portfolio. Something's not right. What do you do? Grab the office copy of Campaign; nip off to the coffee bar around the corner and flick through the back pages, right? Maybe.

Then again, maybe not. Maybe now's the time to think again.

Marketing – that's advertising, design, whatever you want to call it – is changing. It's changing rapidly, completely and irrevocably. What's more, it's changing for the better. Old school ways are just that: old school. New ways of thinking mean new ways of working. New media means a new approach. The days of the 30-second TV ad as creative Holy Grail are over. All those apocryphal stories you heard about advertising are just that: dusty old legends. The eighties are over. Thank God.

Figure 0.2
Cutting edge snowboarding website
www.usbx.co.uk.

Figure 0.3
Kasia Korczak's website for French commercials
production company, La Pac, www.pac.fr.

Figure 0.4
Chloe George's contemporary Brownies' website,
www.chloegeorge.co.uk.

However, tales of marketing's demise have been greatly exaggerated. There's another world out there. A brave new world. It's a fresh, vibrant, intelligent place where talent is recognised and nurtured. Where account people understand and believe in the brands they work on. Where clients are smart, reasonable people. And where creative people have a stake in how, where and why their talents are applied.

This is new wave marketing. It's not confined to TV advertising or billboard posters. It's smart enough to understand that ideas are currency – that they live and breathe in their own right, whether they appear on a 48-sheet billboard in the middle of Piccadilly Circus, a drinks coaster in a bar, an SMS message on a mobile phone or a banner ad on a website. Smart marketing people – be they creatives, suits or anything in between – understand that ideas are the life force of this industry and, as such, ideas are the only thing that can save it from any of its perceived threats: decreasing advertising budgets, recession, anti-globalisation, consumer indifference and so on. Understand that ideas are what we all get up for every morning, ideas are what pay our salaries and ideas are what will define our careers and – if the ideas are good enough – our lives.

So the industry's changing. Which means new roles for creative people. New ways of working. Wider job definitions. Different ways of applying skills. Broader responsibilities. Better rewards. And new ways of working mean new ways of getting that work. Which is where this book comes in. A new game means

INCREASINGLY, PEOPLE ARE GOING TO BE RESPONSIBLE FOR GETTING THEMSELVES WORK, AS CREATIVE DEPARTMENTS ARE OUT-SOURCED.

new rules. Sure, you can call up creative directors' PAs, hassle recruitment people and send off CVs ad infinitum. But in an industry that's defined by innovative, intelligent, clear and direct thinking, there are new ways to get your foot in the door. Wherein lies our first key point: think carefully about which doors you want to get your foot into. Think carefully because some of them are new, some of them are small, some of them take a little work to find. The irony is that often, the smaller the door, the bigger the ideas. Often, the harder it is to find, the more worthwhile it is to seek out.

So, while a degree in English Literature won't necessarily get you into creative marketing, neither will a snowboard and wraparound shades. Today's industry is about smart thinking, not qualifications, fashion sense or any of the other ephemeral and clichéd prerequisites. The days of value judgements are over. What really innovative, creative agencies are looking for today is creative thinkers whose talents can cross media boundaries. Who can come up with great strategies as quickly as they can come up with great executions. Pigeonholes are out; widescreen thinking is in.

The pages ahead form a guide of sorts. We hope it is useful to you. Indeed, we hope the guide gives you direction and inspiration. That it leads you to the right place for you within the industry. That it contributes to what will be a full and fulfilling career. As we were researching and writing this book, wherever we went and whoever we spoke to, three clear points came shining out.

1. It's all about the work. Clever ideas and gimmicks can get you a meeting; only talent and commitment will get you a job.
2. Cut through. The competition's tough out there. How are you going to get yourself noticed?
3. Creativity is a powerful gift. Don't waste it.

Good luck!
Matt Perry and Ant Melder

Marketing Your Creativity was created to provide an overview of some of the more progressive entities on the new marketing landscape and how those agencies work, what kind of work they do and – centrally to this book – how you go about getting work with them. We've spoken to them about what they look for in new employees and what kind of approaches impress them. We've given examples of ideas and inspiration that will serve as a starting point, and show you what it takes to make it absolutely impossible for a creative director not to pick up the phone and call you. Mainly we've looked at digital ways of opening doors, not because it is the only way, but because the medium is fresh, new and offers a world of possibilities. However, as ever with the creative industry, the only real constraint is your own imagination! Also, visit the Marketing Your Creativity website at www.avabooks.ch/avaguides/marketingyourcreativity/. The book has been set out in such a way that design elements help you absorb its content quickly and easily.

ICONS

These graphic symbols are used to identify the four sections of the book. As you read you'll know exactly where you are and to what general topic the content of each page relates to.

TEXT

The text explains the concepts in detail. The text is designed to be imminently readable with the minimum of jargon so that you can quickly and easily embrace the ideas and apply them to marketing yourself creatively.

TIPS

Tips are ideas that will help make your approach to marketing yourself more efficient and creative.

IMAGES

The images featured in this book come from a range of sources and vary in type: photographs, screen shots and print-based images to name a few. Their function is to provide visual examples of the concepts explained in the text.

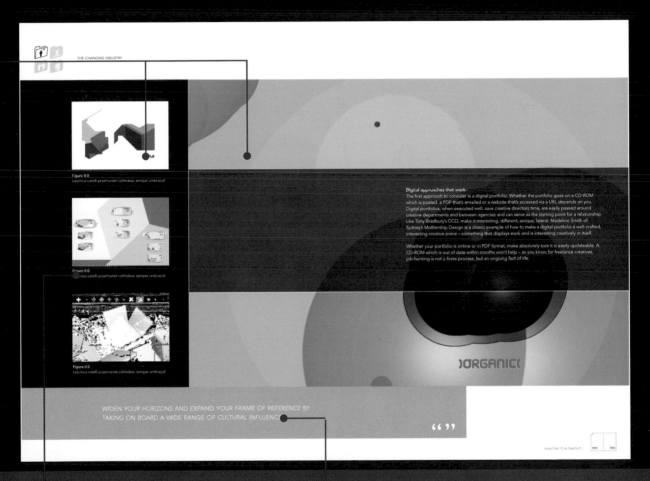

CAPTIONS

The text in the captions expands on what the images are about and why they have been included in this publication.

QUOTES

Often a phrase, or sentence is quoted to emphasise an important idea so that you can quickly understand the gist of a page's content.

CONTENT

01 The changing industry
- The creative department is dead, long live creativity
- A new landscape, a new way of working
- Cut through and stand out
- Making technology work for you

We begin our guide to marketing yourself within the creative industry by putting the industry into context. Central to this debate is the growth over the last 10 years of digital media – and the attitudes of differing agencies towards it. The chapter gives the views of some of the world's most progressive agencies on the impact digital media has had – and will continue to have – on the industry. We explore the changing ways in which people are consuming media – particularly the ways in which technology is enabling marketers to get their message out more quickly, to a wider audience. Examples of some digital routes to getting work and some interesting digital campaigns start to give an idea of how freelance creatives can use technology – and how the industry is using it.

This debate leads on to a look at the evolution of the creative department – and what new wave agencies are looking for in creatives today. By providing insights from agency professionals, we are able to give freelance creatives a firm steer on the kind of talents and abilities in demand today.

By providing an overview of the industry and taking a broad look at the marketing landscape, this chapter enables creatives to consider their role within it. Throughout the chapter, we give the points of view of industry insiders, notable examples of relevant work and some ideas and inspiration for moving forward.

02 Demonstrate your talent
- Understanding the zeitgeist
- You are a brand
- Use digital media to communicate your brand

In this chapter we take a look at what it means to be a creative. We talk about the kind of attributes required to be successful in the job and the foundations readers need to lay to find work. Firstly, this involves understanding and immersing yourself in the zeitgeist. Every agency featured in the book is looking for creatives who go out into the world and make a mark, an impact, a discovery; creatives who get involved in the contemporary culture in which the industry operates and then bring some insight to the table. Some of the creatives featured have done exactly that.

The specific advice offered is varied, but the message is the same: bring us a new perspective, a new way of looking at and solving problems. The competition for work is tough – and getting tougher – but smart, fresh thinking is always in demand. Treating yourself as a brand is a concept which is key to this chapter. Freelance creatives need to take this approach and understand that everything you do will have an impact on the 'brand of you'. In a way the 'brand of you' is the most important brand any creative ever works on. Like any brand, to achieve recognition and success, it needs to be strategically and creatively thought out.

03 Build relationships
- Build and maintain a network
- Using digital media to your advantage
- The power of collaboration

Whatever level readers are at, this chapter and its message are of equal relevance. The point is that the industry is all about building relationships. Whether you're a dedicated freelancer or using freelance as a stepping stone to permanent work, the ability to build relationships is absolutely imperative.

By making this clear, we start to demonstrate to readers what they need to do to find work in the industry. The concept of relationship-building begins the day you decide you want to be a creative. Whether that's at school, college or later on, the key is to take the initiative, starting as early as possible to build and maintain your network – a network of relationships that will last a lifetime. We look at – with some outstanding examples – the power of collaboration.

We also look at various ways in which digital media can play a key part in the process, such as email campaigns and e-zines. We analyse, using examples and the viewpoints of industry insiders, the impact that different digital approaches can have.

04 Get your foot in the door

- Problem solving is a valuable skill
- Prepare to diversify
- Build more relationships
- Don't forget about ideas

This is the key aim of every freelance creative looking to build their profile and client roster. It is that invaluable thing in the industry: an opportunity. In this chapter, we look at how to cultivate these opportunities, how to prepare for them and how, most of all, to be ready when they come your way.

Central to the chapter is the idea that being a 'creative' is a much broader role than it was ten years ago. Because the skill base agencies are looking for in creatives has widened significantly over the last decade, your approach needs to be carefully thought out. In addition to coming up with great ideas, agencies are looking for creatives to work across different media and think strategically. Freelance creatives need to be versatile enough to think and work in whatever media is best for the brand – from print campaigns to digital to direct mail to corporate sponsorship. As a freelance resource, creatives need to demonstrate this ability as early as possible in the relationship. In today's industry, lazy thinking is out and sharp thinking is very much in.

Figure 0.5
A still from Venla Kivilahti's website, www.venla.net.

01 THE CHANGING INDUSTRY

THE OLD DAYS OF THE 30-SECOND TV AD AS THE DEFAULT MEDIUM ARE OVER AND THAT'S HAVING A HUGE IMPACT ON THE WAY CREATIVITY IS APPLIED.

Exactly how are creative departments changing?

'In the future, there won't be such a thing as a creative department. If there is, it will be much smaller,' says Mark Whelan of Cake, London. Cake is one of the new wave agencies which are blurring the lines between creative disciplines, agency department responsibilities and job specifications. In stark contrast to the traditional ad agency above-the-line solution of TV and press ads, Cake are just as likely to deliver an event, a PR campaign or a product redesign as they are an ad campaign. The thinking is open-ended and outside of traditional industry boundaries – which is why the approach to the way the work is done is different. No notions of the 'creative' being done exclusively by the creative department and the 'account handling' being done by the account handlers here.

Mark Whelan continues: 'when I worked in an agency, the idea of a creative department seemed like nonsense to me. The whole place has to be creative, then ideas really can come from anywhere.' The old days of the 30-second TV ad as the default medium are over and that's having a huge impact on the way creativity is applied. 'Traditional media is becoming increasingly irrelevant to young people who are now spending more time doing other stuff rather than watching telly,' Whelan continues.

Figure 1.0
Cake's 'recession buster' poster poked fun at the 'everything must go' sale ethos.

Figure 1.1
When Evian sponsored Kylie Minogue's tour, Cake produced this simple, effective promotional bottle.

"

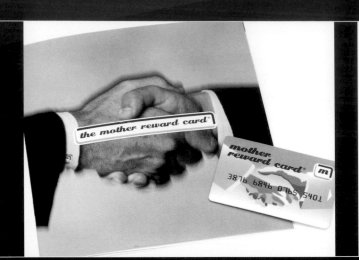

Figure 1.2
The Mother Reward Card: putting a very 'Mother' spin on the loyalty
card phenomenon, www.motherlondon.com.

The rise of digital media and the advent of digital agencies have both contributed to a re-evaluation of the way ideas are conceived and executed. The result is a smaller, sharper, more streamlined creative department which means broader job specifications, more responsibilities, a new attitude to working with clients and a greater focus on results. What this means in reality is that creative departments are shrinking in size. They're less isolated and exclusive. From the biggest multinational network agencies to the smallest hot shops, creative departments are changing, evolving, diversifying. For years, creative departments have been an untouchable force, a magical, mystical place with the exclusive rights to clever, lateral thinking. With the debunking of this myth is coming the new wave of creative thinking. It's thinking like Mark Whelan's that says ideas can come from anywhere and anyone. It's thinking that says 'why have an actual department sectioned off to come up with ideas when the whole place should be coming up with ideas?' How this works in practice depends on which agency you talk to. Of Cake, Mark Whelan says: 'We don't have a creative department but a bunch of creative-thinking people fulfilling different roles…a group of people who excel in creative ways and who are professionals in different disciplines.'

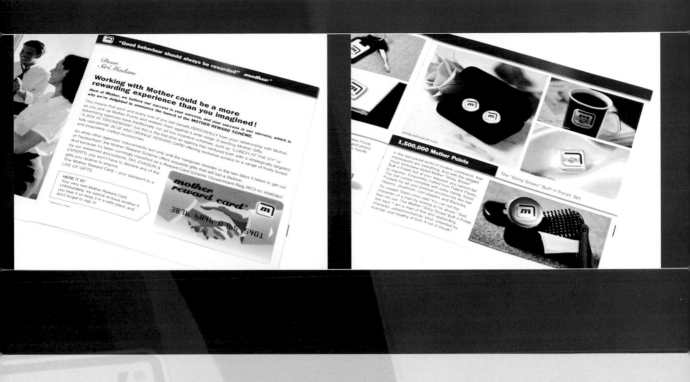

These ideas about the reshaping and restructuring of creative departments are growing, starting to take shape and have an effect on traditional agency set-ups and hierarchies. Another factor having a huge impact on the industry is the burgeoning demand for results-focused work. The importance of industry awards and creative kudos, while partly acknowledged by many clients, is understandably not at the top of their shopping lists when looking for an agency. Mother (London) is one of the younger creative agencies which, due to its structure and philosophy, understands and responds to these needs – while producing some of the best creative work around. Whether by design or simply by the nature of the work, there's a strong, independent air around the agency. Mark Waites was one of the three creatives and a strategist who set the agency up. They did so to focus the emphasis on creativity and move it away from account handling. Waites says, 'we wanted to be our own bosses. We questioned the contribution we could make to the industry – we felt we could do it without account people and that creatives could be responsible for everything.'

So far, it's been a philosophy that's been successful for Mother. The focus on creativity has delivered great work and outstanding results. The latter is enormously important to the agency. It ensures Mother isn't seen as an airy-fairy boutique, but as a heavy duty, results-focused team. This objective is reflected in the way the creatives think and work – and in the kind of people Mother employs in the first place. Mark Waites says: 'Good creatives love to see sales go up. We want results-orientated people…people who are interested in the bottom lines as well as the creative.'

Figure 1.3
This outstanding website was a key part of the marketing campaign for
the brilliant film 28 Days Later, www.28dayslaterthemovie.co.uk.

This is the first lesson for any aspiring young creative or client roster-building freelancer. Great creative work isn't great creative work unless it gets great results. Clients have always insisted that this is the case and agencies, rather than paying lip service to the fact, are starting to truly wake up to it. The growth of digital marketing and the resurgence of direct marketing – two highly measurable media – underline the fact. The industry is remodelling itself around results. Demonstrate your understanding of that fact and your ability to think in those terms and you've already got your nose in front of the competition.

The evolving structure of the creative department and the industry's stronger focus on results are having an impact on the way people are brought into the industry, the way careers develop and grow – and the way you think about yours.

The rise of the freelance creative

Today's smaller, sharper creative agencies are evolving at a much quicker rate than the big multinational network agencies. Their use of freelance creatives enables them to react faster to client demands, to provide some of the best creative talent around, without the huge overhead-associated costs that have traditionally come with it.

Meanwhile, freelance contracting is also becoming increasingly popular within the bigger agencies, as they scale down in line with clients' demands for transparency and value-for-money. Mother is a good example. 'We've been set up to deliver creative ideas through a centralised creative department and then work with specialists to deliver the execution in each channel.' As Tim Heyward of What If? says: 'Increasingly, people are going to be responsible for getting themselves work, as creative departments are out-sourced.'

The move towards creatives working for themselves and cherry-picking projects at different agencies, empowers them. This shows in their work and their attitude to the industry. 'It will be dangerous to train to be an advertising creative in the future,' believes Mark Whelan.

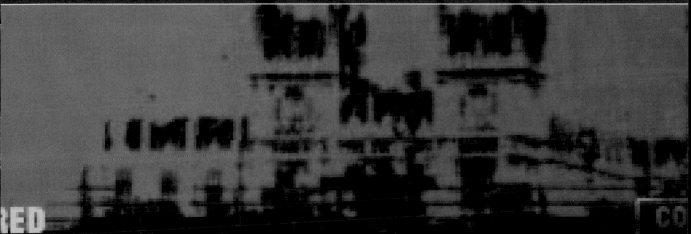

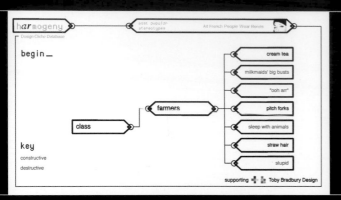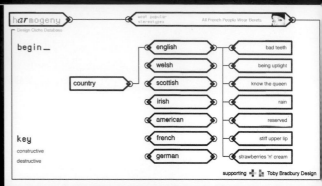

Figure 1.4
Pages from Toby Bradbury's satirical Design
Cliché Database (DCD), www.geocities.com/toby_bradbury/.

TIP – Use your core talent as a base from which to think about a wide range of creative and media solutions.

What kind of person are the best agencies looking for?

So, freelance creatives are a growing breed. But what kind of people are in demand? Mark Waites is very specific about the kind of people his agency looks for. 'Disciplined, responsible creatives who can work on all aspects of the business,' he says. In fact, responsibility is a recurring theme. Tim Heyward at What If?, one of the UK's leading new product development companies, says: 'Old school creatives who turn up to catch the plane to a shoot and have forgotten their passport or who skulk around the creative department being "creative" are not relevant anymore. The industry needs people who are buttoned-down and organised.' And, in addition to this sense of responsibility, agencies need open minds. 'We look for creatives who are open to multimedia – people who aren't just thinking about ads, but all the communication channels,' says Mark Waites.

Strong opinions are another priority. A good example is Toby Bradbury. A young interactive designer, Toby showcased his multimedia talents on his Design Cliché Database (DCD), hosted on his website. The DCD takes a sharp, sometimes satirical look at the work and inspirations of designers. Toby says: 'I believe that designers, far from breaking down stereotypes, reinforce them in order to make the world we inhabit easier to digest. This DCD helps designers to find the stereotypes they need, much like the image banks used in the industry.'

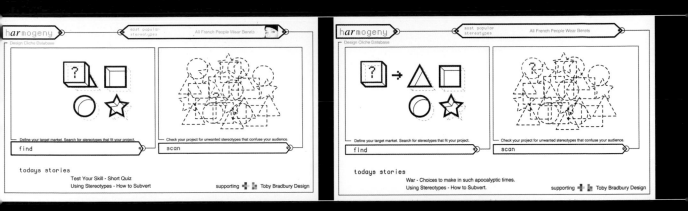

Figure 1.5
The Sunday Times' 'Be Distracted' promotional campaign.

Toby's views on design and branding are forthright: 'as consumers, we have grown savvy to even the more subtle forms of advertising on television. Likewise, television strives to get things across without ramming them down our throats. Look at the current branding for Channels 1, 3 and 5 and you get a load of people "just living" or "dancing" to get across the gist of what these huge corporations are trying to say. But don't get me started on that...the fact that so many phone companies and Internet service providers sell their product as "life" itself, and do it so transparently, shows a real lack of ideas. Nowadays Playstation is having mini-books fall out of magazines, and cartoon strips in the papers promoted the film 28 Days Later. People need to be grabbed in a place they didn't think they would be. At this stage the people who design and think only within their boundaries fall flat on their face. They didn't question what could have been done and so they stuck with poster campaigns and typical marketing methods…'

A campaign of interactive self-promotion – of which the DCD was an integral part – lead to Toby being given the opportunity to work with the BBC as an interactive designer. It's an excellent example of taking a single talent – in this case, design – and using it as a base from which to evaluate other creative forms, to think about a wide range of creative and media solutions.

BE DISTRACTED

THE SUNDAY TIMES

Figure 1.6
Cake found another witty way
to market themselves with this
promotional T-shirt.

Where do I fit in?

Good question. The first thing to do is discard your preconceptions about the industry. For starters, being a creative is no longer about finishing college, getting a job in the creative department of a big agency, putting your feet up and perusing the occasional brief. Creative work – especially as a freelancer, with multiple deadlines and various levels of self-organisation to get on top of – is a hands-on, high-pressure job. But the rewards can be great. Think about where your core talents lie – and what you'd like to do with them. Advertising? Design? Illustration? Digital work? It's good to specialise, but remember; today's industry is about crossing boundaries and stretching the media limits. Consider collaborations and how you can leverage the diverse skills of friends and associates. The illustrators' collective Peepshow (www.peepshow.org.uk) is an excellent example. Combining traditional illustrators' talents with Web design, the site is an interactive gallery of outstanding illustration work. James-Lee Duffy, one of Peepshow's illustrators, used the site as a springboard to work with Cake, London.

Figure 1.1
When The Independent on Sunday magazine did a piece on 'guerrilla marketing', it focused heavily on Cake.

SOMETHING
IN THE
COFFEE

HOW 'GUERRILLA' ADVERTISERS
CONTROL OUR MINDS

THE SUNDAY REVIEW

THE INDEPENDENT
ON SUNDAY

13·FEBRUARY 2000

Figure 1.8
Work by James-Lee Duffy, www.peepshow.org.uk.

A huge fan of street art – anything from graffiti to hand-made signs – and sub-culture art, fashion and music, James-Lee pools his interests into his work. 'I'm always taking photos around the streets,' he says. 'And I'm a big collector of trainers – I've got a pair of 1974 Nike – mint; I collect toys from things like Batman, The Planet of the Apes, Kubrick, Japanese monsters, even Masters of the Universe! I also love artists like Kaws, Espo and Future: I buy anything they produce, from artwork to books. All this stuff really drives me in my work.'

James-Lee is an excellent example of how using your life as inspiration for your creativity can bring results. Using Peepshow as a creative springboard, he has worked for clients including Nintendo, Rizla and the band NU. And he intends to keep exploring his creativity. 'I want to work in New York for a year after Cake, working for a design studio or creative agency, while still doing my illustration in the studio and on the street. Long term I would love to have a studio and work for special clients in London and America. I just want to push myself and still do my artwork – I love it!'

Figure 1.9 & 1.10
Grab their attention: some of James-Lee Duffy's work
from the Peepshow website, www.peepshow.org.uk.

GOOD CREATIVES LOVE TO SEE SALES GO UP.

Which skills are in demand?

You've probably heard industry talk of these being bad times for creatives and work in the creative sector. While client spending on marketing activity is undoubtedly down and permanent jobs in the industry have suffered, freelance is a more buoyant area. The fact that it's tougher to get work simply means that the ways you go about it need to be that much smarter. The answer to the question 'which skills are in demand?' is smart thinking across creative boundaries and media. Naturally, not everyone can be an illustrator or photographer or Web designer. But you need to be thinking in these differing media channels. Your creative solutions need to be all encompassing, not limited to narrow areas of execution. Some skills will always be in demand – great photography; some will become popular for a while before the demand levels off – Web design; some will be less marketable for a while before re-emerging – illustration. The key is to keep honing your skills, keep making contacts, keep building your portfolio and keep expanding your range. Avoid pigeonholes. Remember, it's good to specialise and pick up lots of work in one area, but it doesn't take long to become known as a designer who only does brochures, a copywriter who only writes banner ads, or a photographer who only shoots black-and-white stills. Try to use your expertise and popularity in one area to expand into others. This multiplies the opportunities for work manifold and enables you to keep working when one area of work quietens down.

How do client requirements drive workflow?

It's happened to every freelancer who's been in the business for a while. Workflow is excellent; you're picking and choosing projects; rates are high. The next few months look rosy. Suddenly one project finishes, the next gets cancelled, other work is postponed or put on the backburner and things don't look so great. Rather than fielding phone calls from agencies and juggling work, you're calling up agencies and chasing work, putting in quotes for projects that never get off the ground and doing work on spec for the promise of a larger contract around the corner. Obviously it's important to plan ahead, but as you well know, a large percentage of the future is 'unplannable'. That's the nature of freelancing, part of the attraction and, unfortunately, part of the downside. While one business sector is growing, there can be lots of work. When that growth period ends or slows down, work can dry up. Telecommunications accounts are a good example. While new technologies such as broadband are launched, agencies are busy and the freelance market is buoyant. Once the launch period is over, workflow can slow down and the need for freelancers dies down. Reading the trade press and business media can give you a broad idea of which sectors are busy. An interest in clients' businesses makes your job more enjoyable; a broad economic knowledge gives you an advantage when you're looking for freelance work. Is the IT industry doing well? The financial sector? Are automotive manufacturers launching new cars? Your research enables you to tailor your portfolio or new business presentations to position yourself where the work is.

TIP – *Use your expertise and popularity in one area – one sector or industry – to expand into others.*

Figure 1.11
Sharp, concise, attention-grabbing:
de-construct's website, www.de-construct.co.uk.

IT'S ALL ABOUT GETTING ATTENTION AND IF I SEE A REALLY LONG
EMAIL I MIGHT NOT HAVE TIME TO LOOK AT IT…

...wide range of experience – design, new media, advertising a
strategy – to create a new kind of creative agency.

The seven founding partners had worked together at the no
new media agency Deepend. They believe passionately in o
work for clients that share their vision of communications in
digital media.

01.01.

FRED FLADE, DE-CONSTRUCT " "

Do your research

Whoever you approach for work and however you approach them, make sure you do your research. Find out about the kind of work they do and the kind of culture they foster. Always be looking a year down the track for new industry trends, new opportunities, new ways to implement your talents and the skills you are constantly learning.

For example, which clients does the agency you're approaching have? Do they have one main client and several smaller ones? What kind of work do they do for their clients – ad campaigns, brochures, websites, and digital campaigns? Is the agency focused on one specific medium or are they 'full service'? Have they won any awards for their work? Tim Heyward of What If? says researching the people you are seeing for potential work is crucial: 'Do massive amounts of research into the people you are seeing. Knowledge of someone else's "fame" is very flattering. In addition teach someone something that they did not know.'

Research is a fundamental aspect of your job. Go beyond the trade press – Campaign, Creative Review, Design Week, etc. – and make sure you read everything from D&AD annuals to foreign design books, award catalogues to industry websites. The more you know, the wider your frame of reference, the more hireable you make yourself.

Consider the competition

An integral part of your research is looking at the work other people in your field – and related fields – are doing. Creative work is all about being inspired: by the world, by your environment, by the people and things around you. In a creative sense it's important to be aware of other people's work. On a logistical level, it's essential that you're aware of what the competition is doing. If you're a designer, what kinds of design styles are currently popular? How are other designers going about getting work? Are other designers showing digital portfolios while you trudge around with your 'real' portfolio? Are you a copywriter making unsuccessful phone calls while other writers are using email newsletters to spread the word about their services?

Speak to people: to other freelancers in your field; freelancers in other creative fields; to permanent staff in agencies. What kinds of approaches are popular and successful? If you're a copywriter, perhaps a designer can give you the inspiration for an interesting way of getting work. If you're a designer, perhaps a copywriter could inspire you. Fred Flade at de-construct, a leading London-based cross-media creative agency understands that getting noticed is a problem, because of the volume of applications for jobs and work that most agencies get. He says: 'there are different reasons why certain people stand out. Consider the potential audience. Keeping it short and focused is an immediate advantage. It's all about getting attention and if I see a really long email I might not have time to look at it. One good paragraph and a link to a website is plenty, the portfolio will do the rest.'

TIP – *Speak to other freelancers in your field and freelancers in other creative fields about what kind of approaches for work have been successful.*

While you think about the right approach, remember that what is successful for the competition may not work for you. For example, one copywriter might rely on a business card and word of mouth; another might produce a self-branded monthly newsletter with links to interesting Web articles. Both approaches are valid for those individuals. So while it's important to look at what other people are doing, it's mainly so that you can try to do something better.

Think ahead of the game

When you're putting together your new business presentation, in addition to delivery media and creative execution, think ahead in terms of timelines. Who will receive your communication and when? What will your next step be and when? Will you follow up with an email later today or a phone call tomorrow? Staying on top of the organisational side of things increases your chances of getting work. De-construct's Fred Flade says: 'taking a different approach is good. Usually people simply send an email with a link or CV attached. Breaking the mould usually gets people's attention. A student recently sent me a poster, then after two days I got an email referring to the poster. She was clearly playing with my curiosity and it worked.'

Fred underlines the need for work approaches to be buttoned-down technically as well as cutting-through creatively: 'Surprisingly, some of the applications we receive link to sites that don't work or present broken links. Obviously this is an immediate turn-off. So, if somebody is using an online portfolio, they need to make sure it performs absolutely perfectly on any system and browser.' He also stresses the need to develop and target your approach well: 'Applications that feel as if they have been sent blindly to a whole bunch of people and haven't been addressed specifically aren't good.'

Figure 1.12
Isaac Wong's interactive questionnaire-based website work.

Different ways of communicating

So, the industry is changing rapidly, competition for work is tougher than ever and you need a way to get yourself and your work noticed; a way to make it absolutely impossible for creative directors not to clear some space in their jam-packed diaries to meet you. This is where innovative thinking can give you the edge. And that's where this book can help.

What kind of approach should you take? The formats and technical specifications are as infinite and open-ended as the medium itself. The central issue is the angle of your approach. Exactly how do you impress prospective employers? 'Surprise them with an insight or idea for their business that's on the money,' says Dan Douglas of de-construct, London.

For example, Isaac Wong, a Singapore-based designer, has developed a website which gives the user 'seven steps to making the world a better place'. A surprising, interactive questionnaire-based website, the work uses the interesting premise that it's not Wong who provides the answers – the seven steps – but the user themselves. 'As there are no absolute rights or wrongs on how to create a better world, the site attempts to use seven universal values as a discussion ground to stimulate users into thinking and forming their own opinions on improving the world,' Wong explains. It's thought-provoking work.

So, think about what you want your communication to achieve. Are you looking for a quick-hit that demands attention and a phone call? Are you seeking to draw attention to a piece of work you've done or some PR you've generated? Or are you playing a longer game, with an eye on building a relationship?

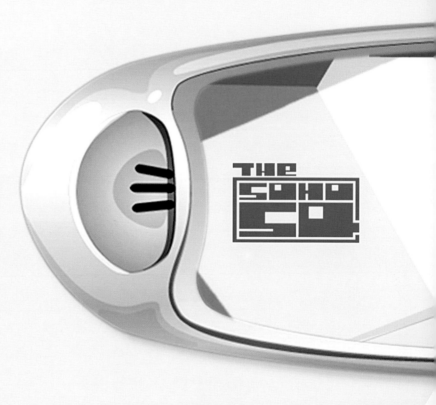

Figure 1.13
Soho Square by Benji
Wiedemann.

Figure 1.14
Benji Wiedemann's personal logo is designed to represent the complexity of visual communication.

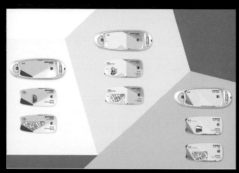

Figure 1.15
Soho Square: an interactive city guide for Soho, designed and developed by Benji Wiedemann.

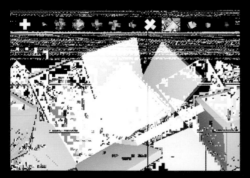

Figure 1.16
Testbox: one of a series of ten-second music animations created by Benji Wiedemann, to synchronise sound to visuals.

WIDEN YOUR HORIZONS AND EXPAND YOUR FRAME OF REFERENCE BY TAKING ON BOARD A WIDE RANGE OF CULTURAL INFLUENCES.

Digital approaches that work

The first approach to consider is a digital portfolio. Whether the portfolio goes on a CD-ROM which is posted, a PDF that's emailed or a website that's accessed via a URL depends on you. Digital portfolios, when executed well, save creative directors' time, are easily passed around creative departments and between agencies and can serve as the starting point for a relationship. Like Toby Bradbury's DCD, make it interesting, different, unique, lateral: something that displays work and is interesting creatively in itself.

Whether your portfolio is online or in PDF format, make absolutely sure it is easily updatable. A CD-ROM which is out of date within months won't help – as you know, for freelance creatives, job-hunting is not a finite process, but an ongoing fact of life.

)ORGANIC(

" "

Figure 1.17
Stills from Venla Kivilahti's 'Phantasmal Voyage'
interactive digital video, www.venla.net.

Cutting through with film and animation

The question isn't 'why?', but 'why not?'. If you've created an animation or short film, the next step is to get it seen. But make sure it's short, attention-grabbing (and attention-holding) and easy to download. And make sure that – unless this really is your specialist area – you don't get pigeonholed as an animation expert with no other design skills. Finnish interactive designer Venla Kivilahti's work is a good reference point. In her short, animated film 'Feeling for all the People', she sets out her vision for a new everyday service at train stations. Platform musicians provide 'uncommercial refreshment' while people wait for their train. Produced in Flash/Premiere, Venla describes the film as being about 'people who come from different backgrounds and have their individual hopes and dreams.'

Venla has used her interest in 'interactive new media and linear animation in terms of storytelling' as a springboard to work within the new media industry. These interests – she even wrote her MA dissertation on the Sandman graphic novel series – have given her marketable skills in the new media industry. She recognises that continual portfolio building is essential for a steady stream of work. It's also clear to her that while animation and a diverse range of new media skills are in demand, traditional design skills remain important. She says: 'my portfolio consists of recent multimedia pieces and people have said they are very creative and unique. Employers, however, would like to see more traditional design pieces there, as well.'

Email campaigns

Email campaigns and e-zines are excellent ways to get noticed and build relationships. But remember, unsolicited emails are often deleted without even being opened; many that are opened are closed and deleted within seconds. So what makes your campaign stand out? How hard is the subject line of your email working? What value are you giving the recipient in return for their attention? Remember, an email that takes a long time to explain itself, is difficult to read or, worse still, boring, is a mark against your name. Make no mistake about it, your next email will be deleted without a second thought. Take a look at some of the examples throughout this book of good digital approaches. Each of the executions was recommended for the book not by the people who created them, but by the industry people who received them – an excellent gauge of their success.

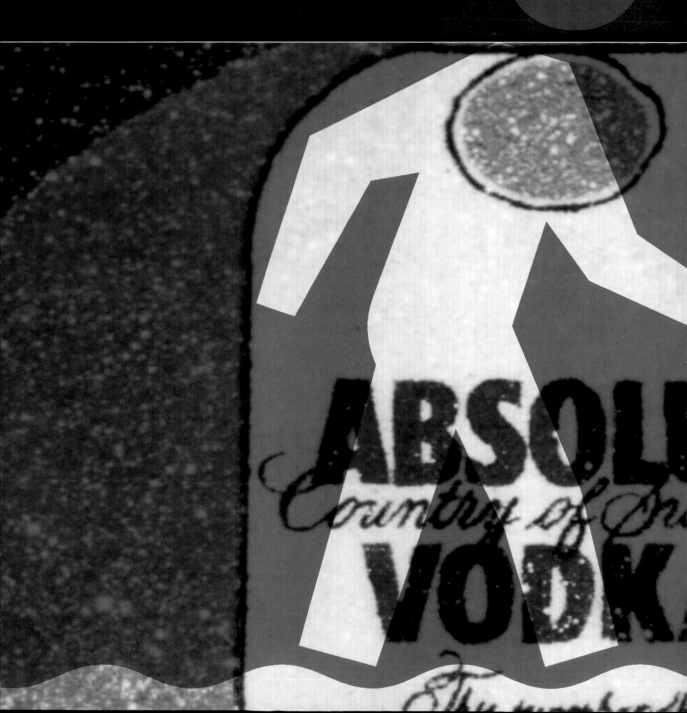

TURNING YOUR TRADITIONAL PORTFOLIO INTO A DIGITAL PORTFOLIO OPENS UP ALL KINDS OF DOORS FOR YOU.

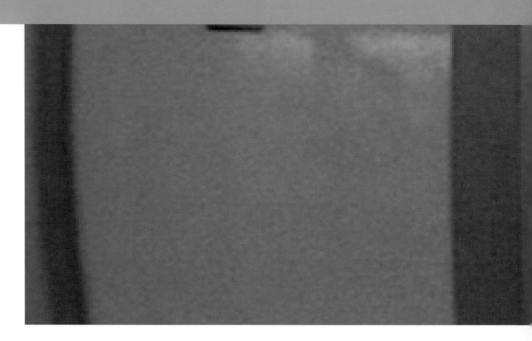

How popular culture impacts on you

As a creative person, your job is to act as a filter. You are the filter through which popular culture passes, is interpreted, developed and understood. Which means that it's your job to have your finger on the pulse of the zeitgeist. Whether you love or hate Big Brother, boy bands, modern car design, New Labour or contemporary architecture, it's your job to have an opinion on it. To be aware of what's happening in the real world – on the streets, in the clubs, on television and, yes, in the charts. As Tim Heyward says: 'Creatives need to have a gut level appreciation of brand, starting with understanding how to market themselves.

There is a growing desire for faster more responsive creatives. Old-fashioned creatives are trying to emulate street culture or "real life" advertising, but they fail because they still rely on high budgets and high production values to recreate what kids are shooting on a digital video camera.'

He continues: 'The adage that only the advertising agency can understand brand and client service is out dated. This is no longer a differentiator. There are kids in Notting Hill who are delivering end-to-end marketing campaigns for their brands.'

" "

usbx presents UNIT

Figure 2.0
Image taken from Alastair Green's website,
www.usbx.co.uk.

Your first task is to decide where you want to be in this moving landscape. Is your core source of work big agencies that use you to interpret the zeitgeist to bring fresh ideas to them? Or do you want to operate closer to the source – be one of these metaphorical 'kids in Notting Hill', working directly for your clients in a new creative sphere and delivering end-to-end solutions?

Whatever you decide, you'll find the way you work and the kind of work you do is evolving to meet consumers' growing cynicism. In Tim Heyward's opinion: 'Not only have "ordinary" people become ad literate and cynical, but the barriers to entry for delivering marketing communications have evaporated. Technology is no longer an inhibitor and whilst "old skool" advertisers are struggling to understand its place, young kids and smart agencies are exploiting it.'

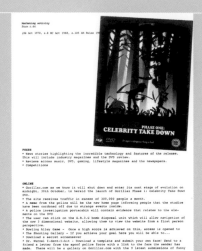
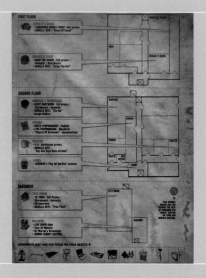

Figure 2.1
Gorillaz's 'Celebrity Take Down' press release, created by
Zombie Flesh Eaters, came in the form of a Police warning letter
with a crime statement and the actual CD in an evidence bag.

BEING A SPONGE MEANS TAKING EVERYTHING IN; BEING OPEN
TO IDEAS AND INSPIRATIONS.

Turning yourself into a sponge

This is the most important thing any creative
can ever learn. It's an absolutely essential part
of the job description: without it, your
creativity will go stale. The whole idea of
creativity is based on a response to the world,
producing a reaction to the events that shape
our lives. Becoming a sponge means walking
around with your eyes open; with your mental
antennae set to 'receive'.

Exactly what should you be looking at, what
information should you be taking in?
Everything that you're interested in – and
everything else too. Inspiration for ideas can
come from an item on the news or an item of
clothing worn by someone on the train. The
spark for a creative solution could come from a
book, a newspaper, an art exhibition, or a
cartoon. It could come from a website or the
design of a beer coaster in the pub, from an
award annual or an Argos catalogue.

Keep your options open. As Tim Heyward says:
'Clients will buy your youth and your
knowledge of the zeitgeist. The best thing that
a young person can do if they want to work in
the creative industry is to go off and be a DJ or
something first.'

Figure 2.2
The actual 'Celebrity Take Down' CD.

Figure 2.3
With its digital work for Gorillaz, Zombie Flesh Eaters has
created a unique, irreverent personality.

THE COMMON TRAIT AMONG PEOPLE WHO WORK HERE IS THAT WE
ALL TRY TO THINK ABOUT EVERYTHING WE DO DIFFERENTLY.

Predicting the future

The flipside of becoming a creative sponge is this: the realisation that everything you see has
already been done; how can you do something else? How can you think beyond the obvious to
deliver something original? It's a question of taking your influences and building something fresh.
That's exactly what the creative team behind the Gorillaz animated band project did. The project
started with the realisation that kids don't just watch television any more – that in this media-rich
age, digital channels are as valid as television. The simple idea of an animated band enabled
traditional channels – pop videos, for example – to be subverted, while delivering more creative
impact through a website.

Tom Thorne is the Business Manager at Zombie Flesh Eaters, the creative design company set up
to deliver the visualisation of the Gorillaz band – and brand. He describes Zombie Flesh Eaters as
'a creative house' and 'facilitator' for all aspects of the Gorillaz visual identity. It's clear that
Zombie understands that in order to reach its audience and make the brand credible it had to
think about new ways of communicating. 'The common trait among people who work here is that
we all try to think about everything we do differently. It doesn't matter if we're making a new
video, adding to the online presence or putting together a press pack – we try to make sure we
get through to people with clever, interesting and witty creative communications.'

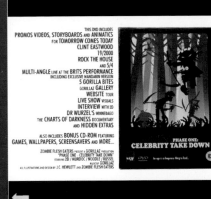

Please extract a positive ID from all sources available.
Once this is done you are authorised to:

> INFORM A COLLEGUE

"

TOM THORNE, ZOMBIE FLESH EATERS

BMWFILMS.COM PRESENTS
BEAT THE DEVIL

Everywhere you look, old ways of marketing are being questioned and rethought. Tim Heyward notes: 'In the nineties BMW would run its highly finished ads in breaks between Prime Suspect, which added a layer of kudos and credibility to the brand and the impression it left in the minds of the audience. How do you do this when the most popular shows on TV are celebrity game shows and reality TV?'

BMW's solution was to assert its brand credibility with its series of films on the Internet. Combining word-of-mouth kudos with the value of working outside of television, with big name directors and stars was a huge success. It's a good example of how a brand can tap into the zeitgeist and use a more direct digital approach to get the message across.

Tim Heyward's take on the future of advertising has specific relevance to creative freelancers: 'What's happening in advertising has already happened in Hollywood. The way the old studio system has been pushed aside is a potential model for the future of advertising agencies. It used to be the studio that made a film, now it is the star or the actor. The role of the studio is to facilitate or create a vehicle that helps the star make the film. Everyone in Hollywood is a freelance consultant with specific skills, which are brought in around a project. This is where advertising is going and the role of the producer is becoming critical.'

TIP – Always be looking a year down the track for new industry trends and opportunities.

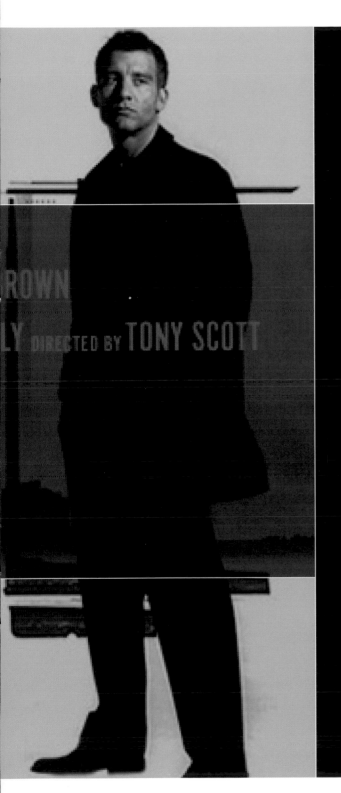

Figure 2.4
Stills from the ground-breaking BMW online film series,
www.bmwfilms.com.

IN A WAY THE 'BRAND OF YOU' IS THE MOST IMPORTANT BRAND ANY CREATIVE EVER WORKS ON.

What do you stand for?

Just as there are many different kinds of agencies – from the creative-led hot-shops to client-led multinationals – there are many different kinds of creatives. As a freelance creative resource, it's important to decide exactly what kind of creative you are and where to position yourself in the market. Probably the best and easiest way to do this is to step back for a minute and think about why you do what you do. Is it because it seems like a good career? Because you're doing what you studied to do? Is it because you want to make lots of money, or because you are passionate about your job? Thinking about exactly why you do your job enables you to evaluate the kind of work you should be doing. It enables you to consider the question 'what do I stand for?' and how the work you do impacts on that.

Thinking about what kind of work you do, what kind of work you want to do and how your personality, ideals and ambitions have an effect will give you an insight into the 'brand of you'. Think about it this way: everything you do will have an impact on the 'brand of you'. In a way the 'brand of you' is the most important brand any creative ever works on. Like any brand, to achieve recognition and success, it needs to be strategically and creatively thought out.

That might start by using talent to get known outside your core area of expertise. By building the brand of you in this way, you can begin to open doors for yourself – doors that lead to future projects. A good example of brand-of-you-building is Dominic Franks, an artist with a unique glitter art style. He negotiated with Absolut Vodka and was commissioned to produce artworks that were exhibited in bars in Soho, London. He was subsequently snapped up to work on projects at Cake. It happened organically: 'I had an exhibition of work in a bar in Soho and Mark from Cake was interested in the work I had done. We talked about my history and the fact that I had used my glitter work and my creativity in events in the past. This work led on naturally to being involved with Cake,' says Dominic.

Figure 2.5
Dominic Franks' Absolut vodka 'glitter' artwork.

“ ”

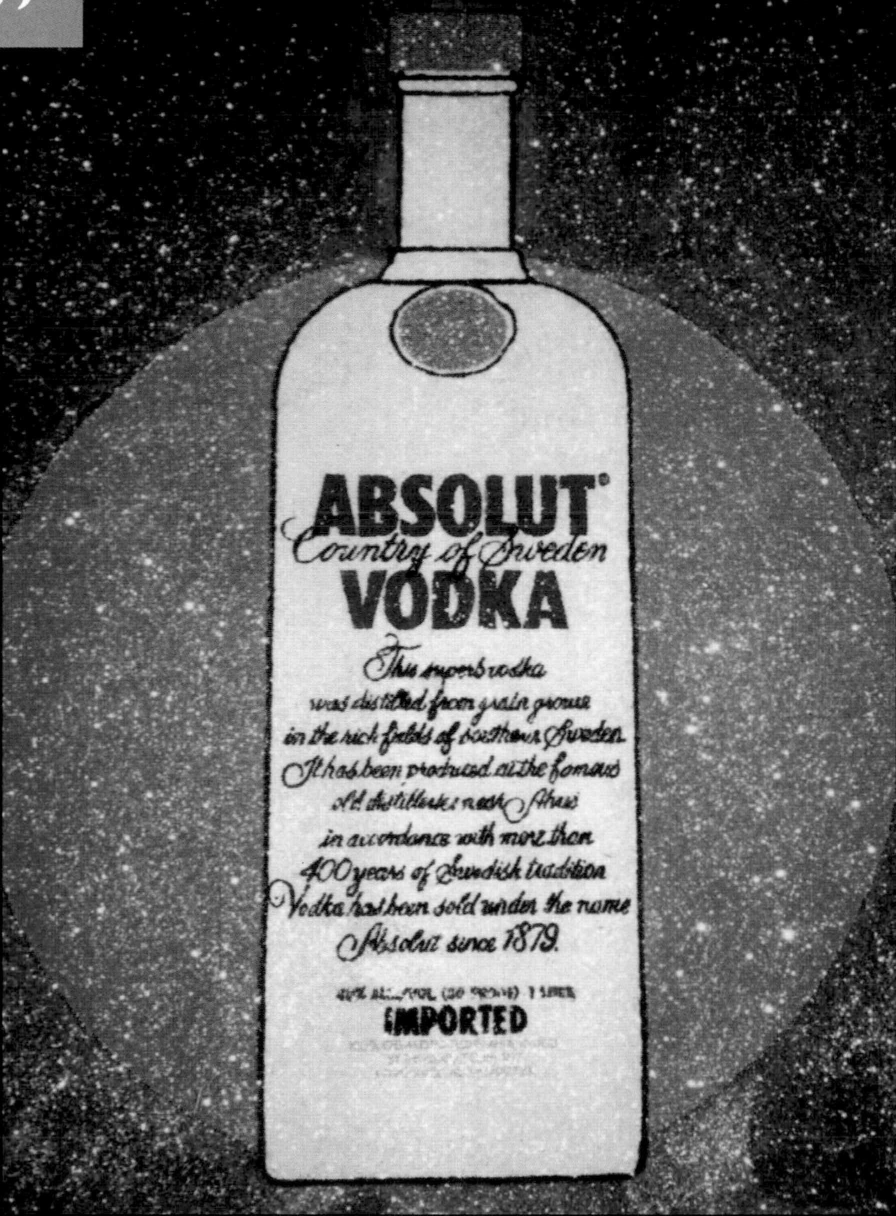
ABSOLUT
Country of Sweden
VODKA
IMPORTED

Figure 2.6
Be unique: Lucy McLauchlan's illustrations
speak for themselves.

DO EVERYTHING YOU CAN TO SET YOURSELF APART, BUT THE GIMMICKY STUFF DOESN'T WORK.

Developing the brand of you

Just as a commercial brand can never stand still, neither can the brand of you. You need to keep honing it, pushing it, growing it. In time, the rewards of brand recognition will come. A good example is Lucy McLauchlan of BEAT13, a music-obsessed creative group of friends based in Birmingham. BEAT13 is, effectively, a space for creativity which has grown into a website and gallery space. After having worked on various projects for BEAT13, Lucy's work was shown to a design group in Tokyo. This lead to an invitation to work in Osaka with a group of UK artists – many from the Scrawl collective.

Another member of the group is Matt Watkins, the inspiration behind BEAT13, who also works with Zombie Flesh Eaters on the Gorillaz project. It was demonstrating the BEAT13 website that opened the door to work on Gorillaz for him. Both Lucy and Matt are excellent examples of the way in which getting your work and talents displayed in a wide range of forums can grow your 'brand' and lead to further projects.

The Web especially has increased the opportunity for your work to be seen and your brand to grow. Use it in every way you can – whether that's through your own website or contributions on other people's websites.

MARK WAITES, MOTHER ‘‘ ’’

'As you go about developing the 'brand of you', remember, once your brand becomes known, you have the ability to affect it negatively as well as positively. Think of every communication, piece of work, phone call and meeting as a piece of brand communication. For example, if you're considering a stunt to get work, consider your approach carefully. Mother's Mark Waites says: 'Do everything you can to set yourself apart, but the gimmicky stuff doesn't work. You get noticed for the wrong reasons. It's a bit like writing the world's most offensive ad: it gets you noticed but ultimately is wrong for the brand.'

Tim Heyward agrees: 'Stunts don't work. Don't over complicate ideas. Don't waste too much time perfecting one execution when you should be showing ten great concepts.'

Evidence of your brand-building skills can also help you get work. Cake's Mark Whelan most definitely looks for these skills: 'I like people who come to me and say things like, "we did a club at university and here is the flyer and the poster and this is the PR that we got."'

 TIP – *Use the Web in every way you can starting with your own website or work on other people's websites.*

Yes... I HAVE done a days work in my life

Are you tired of being accosted at your local working mans club? Do you find your snazzy T-shirts and wicked sense of irony just don't cut it in the queue at the kebab shop?

The answer is in your hands.

Our research showed that 85% of Graphic Designers have never used a shovel, 92% would get an expert round to wire a plug and 30% think 'Sand Paper' was a trendy publication in the early 1990's casting a satirical eye on the Gulf War.

With treatment from us, your smooth, molly-coddled hands will look like you've been wrestling bears, in just 2 Weeks!

Before 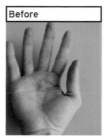 **After Treatment**

FROM PRETTY BOY DAISY PICKER TO GRAPPLING WIFE BEATER IN JUST 2 WEEKS!

CLICK HERE! START TO REGAIN SOME RESPECT!

Figure 2.7
Toby Bradbury has some fun at the expense of 'pretty boy' designers with this subversive digital piece.

TIP – To promote yourself think about using the free Web space being offered by the telecommunications companies to publicise technologies such as broadband.

Achieving brand recognition

Lucy McLauchlan is an excellent example of the benefits of brand recognition. It shows that your work can speak for you, can get your 'proposition' across and deliver future opportunities for you. Think about ways of getting your work and message out there, look for opportunities to showcase your talent. Start small and think creatively. For example, many local councils display local people's work on their websites; many have a space specifically set aside for new, local talent. Local sports clubs and social clubs often have similar spaces on their websites. You could contribute some design work for the sports club site or perhaps write a history of the town for inclusion on the council site.

Also consider free Web space being offered by the telecommunications companies to publicise technologies such as broadband. Look for ways in which you can use this space with little or no expense to get your message out and start building your brand.

Figure 2.8
Happy whatever! Toby Bradbury gives the idea of greeting cards his own unique spin.

Figure 2.9
Isaac Wong's website for Kinetic Interactive, www.kinetic.com.sg.

Figure 2.10
The Singapore Children's Cancer Foundation website, created by Isaac Wong, www.ccf.org.sg.

Websites that reward the user

Websites are an excellent way to demonstrate your talents, communicate your brand and get work. The various disciplines involved – from design to animation to copywriting – provide an excellent creative showcase. The key to using that showcase to maximum effect is to produce a website that rewards the user. Which means a website that delivers a useful, interesting, funny, moving or informative experience. Websites with 'sticky content' – content that holds users' interest and keeps them coming back – are not easy to produce, but they are an excellent way to market your skills. Add value to the user in some way – through interesting links, outstanding design or humour – and creative directors will keep revisiting your site. As your URL is passed around, your brand will grow and work will undoubtedly follow.

Isaac Wong's interactive 'seven steps to making the world a better place' website is a good example. Based in Singapore, Isaac took up Interactive Media Design in Temasek Polytechnic and majored in Electronic Media Design. During his second year in poly, for his internship, he worked with one of Singapore's leading interactive companies, Kinetic Interactive (www.kinetic.com.sg). This lead to work for the Singapore Children's Cancer Foundation website (www.ccf.org.sg), but it's on the 'seven steps…' website that Isaac's key talents really shine (see page 44). The site is an intriguing combination of interactivity and conceptual thinking. It's a good example of how the multi-tasking element of website work can be of benefit by showing you where your core skills lie. Isaac says: 'The project has helped me achieve something I never expected it to. It has helped me to realise something about myself. After completing the project I realised that I'm not really good at graphic design…but stronger in thinking, conceptualising and interactivity.'

Another great website is Alastair Green's snowboarding forum at www.usbx.co.uk. An art director at Ogilvy Interactive, London, Green trained as a traditional graphic designer and worked for a small agency, Steel Design, before joining Ogilvy Interactive at the height of the dotcom years. Green has built an impressive site around this personal interest. The site combines outstanding graphic design, Flash animations and informative reports from members of the USBX snowboarding collective. The pulling together of these elements makes an excellent website – and an excellent brand-building tool for Green. And while he is happy in a permanent position at Ogilvy, he

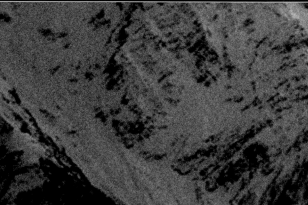

Figure 2.11
Alastair Green's USBX website brilliantly evokes the exhilaration of snowboarding, www.usbx.co.uk.

AS YOU START THINKING ABOUT STRATEGIC WAYS OF MARKETING YOURSELF, SPEAK TO STRATEGISTS, PLANNERS, ACCOUNT PEOPLE AND CLIENTS.

understands the importance of building the 'brand of you' and the strengths of a good website in doing this. He also understands the importance of working across media boundaries. 'I am not afraid to use any medium, be it interactive or more traditional print based to get my message across. Being able to blend advertising thinking with a strong design aesthetic is one of my key strengths.'

The USBX site is just one of the ways in which Green brings his inside and outside work interests together. He says: 'I'm really into video games. You only have to play games like Splinter Cell and Vice City to realise that this is a great medium for creativity. And I like playing

around with stuff on my Mac. The advent of digital media has been great: it allows you to publish your creative thoughts so easily. I can have an idea in the morning and have it finished and published on the net (caffeine willing) by the evening. But, of course, the opposite is true sometimes – and the project will run and run. For example, the first DVD I did took seven months to complete just because I wasn't used to the technology. But I am now.'

When asked where digital technology will lead him within the industry, Green says: 'My own small creative agency…with a service office in the Alps of course.'

" "

Figure 2.12
Gypsies are for real: thought-provoking poster/booklet design by Kasia Korczak.

Figure 2.13
Darkly humorous work for the campaign against drunk driving for INSEAD
business school, Fontainbleau, France. Art directed by Kasia Korczak.
Copywriting by Jim Birmant and Payam Sharifi.

Digital direct mail

Young Polish designer/art director Kasia Korczak is the creative who got de-construct's Fred Flade
interested with her approach. She sent him a poster from one of her latest projects – a 'don't
drink and drive' campaign which comprised posters, flyers and a brand identity. Having aroused
his interest, she followed up with a series of emails. Kasia believes in a highly targeted approach:
'looking for work means approaching each company case by case. It's necessary to do research
on what the company is about and who works there before approaching them. Then put together
a specific cover letter, tailored CV and any additional material you think they'll like.'

Kasia is well versed in working with and for different target audiences. Having gone to school in
Poland, she did a foundation course in photography and fine art there before moving to London
in 1995 to study BA in Fine Art at London Guildhall University. She has worked in motion graphics,
video and photography and has done Web, print, CD-ROM and digital TV design in London and
Paris. Freelancing in London and Paris for the likes of the photographer Alan Clarke
(www.alanclarke.co.uk) and the creative consultancy Bruise Ltd. (www.bruise.ws), has taught Kasia
a lot about a wide range of creative disciplines. How does this affect the way she approaches
getting work and structuring her career? 'I do not plan my future work-wise, as there are too many
little surprises that influence my choice as I go along,' she says. 'There is no certain company or a
plan which I am trying to fulfil. The only thing that is important to me is to keep being involved in
projects on different platforms, to work on projects that continually challenge me. This is why I
worked firstly in photography, then in motion graphics, then print design and interactive design.'

By following this career curve and picking up experience and contacts along the way, Kasia is well
positioned in the evolving creative industry. Her work in a wide range of media channels is a plus
– as is the confidence of having freelanced in different countries.

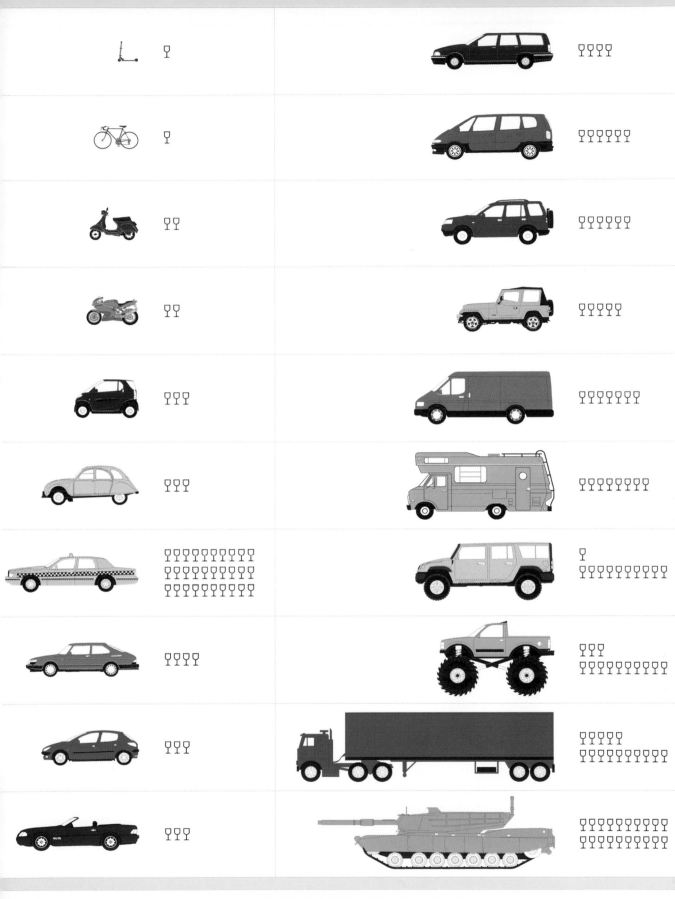

PERMISSIBLE ALCOHOL LEVELS GIVEN VEHICULAR SAFETY

PLEASE NOTE: Consumer trends show a marked increase in vehicles of larger physical stature such as vehicles able to run concurrently on four wheels (4x4), otherwise known as sports utility vehicles (SUV). The marketing of such vehicles revolves primarily around the said vehicles' size as an antidote to danger stemming from a possible collision. Motor vehicles found in the lower and median tonne range—1 to 2 cubic tonnes and 2-3 cubic tonnes respectively—exhibited no additional safety performance when tested in head-on collisions resulting from alcohol-impaired driving. Those vehicles found in the superior tonne range—4 or more cubic tonnes—effectively safeguard the driver and passengers of the said vehicle but may pose mortal danger to other individuals found within a 50 m radius of the collision.

The above figures, save those of the taxi, concern permissible alcohol rates for the driver. However, the illustrations are not based on any factual analysis of the blood-alcohol levels in individual drivers, or the safety features of vehicles belonging to the aforementioned drivers. They do not demonstrate the extent to which alcohol can impair an individual's driving vis-à-vis the type of vehicle s/he drives. The study's findings confirm the hypothesis that individuals aged between 23 and 40 in the Fontainebleau area outside of Paris, France pose a substantial threat to themselves and other individuals when they drink and drive.

Regardless of legal limits, drinking and driving is not safe.

DESIGNATE A DRIVER. USE THE PARTY BUSES OR A TAXI.

LEGEND: ♀ one glass of wine, or the equivalent, consumption per hour.

Be Smart.
Drive Safe.

madelinesmith is mothership
0403 869 989 or madeline@mothership.c

STRUCTURE YOUR PORTFOLIO IN AN ORDER THAT MAKES LOGICAL
SENSE AND GIVES YOU A NARRATIVE STORYLINE TO TALK THROUGH
WHEN YOU PRESENT IT IN PERSON.

Figure 2.14
Madeline Smith's Mothership Design digital portfolio is a
great example of using the medium to its best effect.

Digital portfolios

Whatever other methods you use to get work, the portfolio remains an integral part of the process. Whether a phone call or a clever piece of digital direct mail gets you a meeting for some prospective work, that meeting will be based around your portfolio. Whatever changes affect the industry and whatever new skills are in demand; those skills and talents will always be displayed in a portfolio of some sort. However, that portfolio doesn't necessarily have to be the traditional black zip-up case that you carry from meeting to meeting. This is the age of the digital portfolio.

Turning your traditional portfolio into a digital portfolio opens up all kinds of doors for you in the hunt for work. A digital portfolio can be loaded up online or simply made into a PDF. This enables you to email the URL or the PDF to creative directors who can view your work without you even going in to their studios. While the time-saving element of this process is undoubtedly valuable, as a freelancer, you'll probably agree that there are occasions when it's more useful to meet a prospective client face-to-face. In these cases, presenting your portfolio on a laptop (if you have one) can make an excellent impression.

The key to the successful pitch – in person or by email – of a digital portfolio is making sure the portfolio is well thought out, gives a good flavour of the range of your work, flows well creatively and works without any technical problems.

The digital portfolio of Madeline Smith of Sydney's Mothership Design is an excellent example. Taking the idea of the portfolio as a 'book', as it is known, Madeline has crafted the piece as an actual book that you can flick through digitally. 'Creative work has traditionally been presented in a "book" and I liked the irony of a digital portfolio also appearing in a book format,' she says.

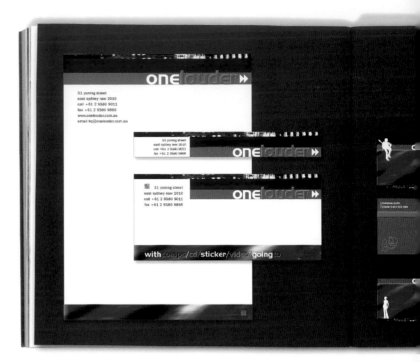

Figure 2.15
How to do it right: pages from the outstanding Mothership Design portfolio by Madeline Smith.

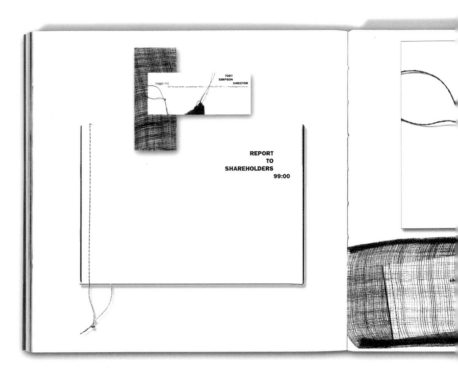

REPORT
TO
SHAREHOLDERS
99:00

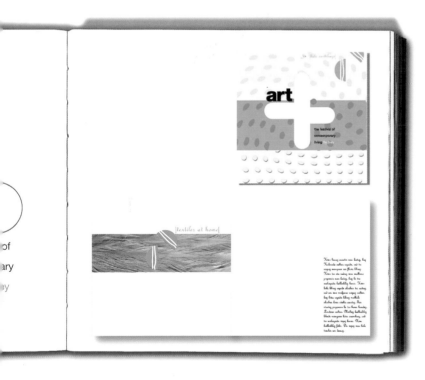

03 BUILD RELATIONSHIPS

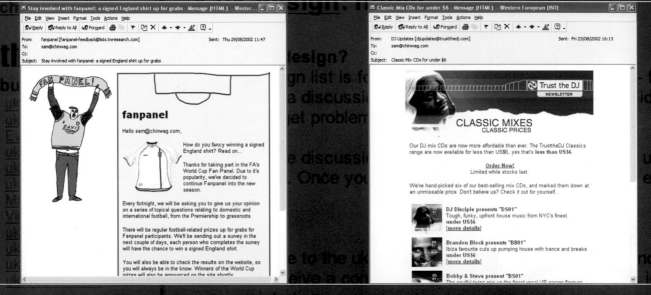

Figure 3.0
Email marketing agency Chinwag delivers three million emails a
month to 15,000 active registered members.

TIP – *Email clients your latest campaigns; send them the URL of your updated website.*

Always be networking

Just as salesmen are traditionally taught to 'always be closing', creative people (and especially freelance creatives) should always be networking. Of all the advice about getting work in this book, this is the most important. The simple fact is that networking is about developing new relationships and new relationships can lead to new work opportunities.

So how should you be networking? And where? You should start with your existing clients. Whether you are currently working with them or not, stay in touch. Email them your latest campaigns. Send them the URL of your updated website. Drop them a phone call. Buy them lunch. However you go about it, ensure that you remain top-of-mind for when big campaigns kick-off. As you know, a one-off client for a one-off project is OK, but the core aim of this business is to build a roster of clients who keep coming back to you regularly.

You should also be looking to expand your network to potential future clients. Get to know agency receptionists and creative directors' personal assistants. Research agencies and people you'd like to work for. Try to get a short period of their time for a meeting to show your portfolio or, if possible, take them out to lunch.

Also, be looking to build relationships outside of the creative industry. Often, talking to family, friends or friends of friends can lead to projects where you work direct for clients. Deliver the best possible service at a good price and you can nurture an excellent long-standing client.

Figure 3.1
Kasia Korczak's beautiful identity design for London-based fashion
photographer Alan Clarke, www.alanclarke.co.uk.

Figure 3.2
Pages from the website of La Pac, the Parisian
commercials production company, www.pac.fr.

Most of all, as you go about building your network of contacts, don't forget to keep building your portfolio. Don't lose sight of doing the kind of work that you are proud of and is beneficial to your brand. Understand what agencies and direct clients need – and keep delivering. This will make your particular skills indispensable and create a need for your services.

An excellent example of using digital channels to aid networking is the email discussion lists run by the email-marketing agency, Chinwag. It was started by the digital marketer Sam Michel, whose background includes working on the launch of the first Time Out magazine online and the Popcorn.com site for Carlton Television. Whilst working in the industry Sam started to put together the foundations of Chinwag – an email that enabled members of the UK's digital marketing community to enter into debates about key industry issues. As the lists and the subject areas evolved, Sam gave up his other work to focus on what had become a full time hobby. Chinwag is now delivering three million emails a month to 15,000 active registered members, as well as delivering email marketing solutions to a range of clients.

'Although the lists themselves will not make us rich, they allow us to build very strong relationships with the wider marketing community – individuals that are interested in a whole range of digital marketing issues. From these relationships we have been able to develop a comprehensive and deep understanding of the email marketing industry. In addition, we are in regular contact with people who could be potential future clients and partners. This regularly leads us to new projects.'

Figure 3.3
Gamoola blend digital design talent with 3D animation skills to create
everything from dangerously addictive games to television visuals. Shown
here is stand-out work for Ms Dynamite, www.gamoola.com.

Start early

Whatever level you are at as you read this book – be it young creative finding your feet in the industry, experienced freelancer or anything in between – this chapter and its message are of equal relevance. The point is very simple, but very important: the creative industry is all about building relationships. Whether you're a dedicated freelancer or using freelancing as a stepping stone to permanent employment, the ability to build relationships is absolutely imperative. Networks of relationships and contacts are what drive the business. The further you go in the industry, the more important the ability to build those relationships becomes. It's as important as the lifeblood of the industry – creative talent itself. Digital media is an outstanding facilitator in this process.

Timing is crucial. Think carefully about not only how, but also when, you contact people. By way of an example, Mark Waites makes an interesting point about students who approach Mother looking for work: 'Timing and establishing a relationship early is critical. In June the phones ring off the hook, which is stupid – creative people need to be creative enough to start establishing relationships months earlier…it can take a year to do this.'

In fact, the concept of relationship building begins the day you decide you want to be a creative. Whether that's at school, college or later on, the key is to take the initiative, starting as early as possible to build and maintain your network – a network of relationships that will last a lifetime. This network of relationships will provide you with the things you need to succeed: help, support, ideas, and – importantly in the context of this book – opportunities for work. Perhaps even more importantly, each relationship can lead to more contacts and further relationships.

Your college friends may later become your colleagues; your tutor may be your career advisor; your first boss may hire you again later in your career…or you may hire your first boss later in your career. The industry thrives on developing careers, people and ideas.

The earlier you start building your network, the wider it will be. Make the effort to keep in touch with your tutors, your peers and your seniors. If you get on well with a client, he or she should become part of your network. Whether each individual contact benefits you directly or not, these are the relationships on which your career will be built.

Wherever you seek out contacts and relationships, digital media can be a great facilitator for the process. The Friends Reunited website is a great example of the way in which digital media can work to keep people in touch. Email in general is an excellent way, too. Just remember, the earlier you establish a contact the better – just like any other relationship, email relationships will get deeper, closer and more mutually beneficial with time.

Figure 3.5
Brilliantly individual: the home page of the Peepshow
website has a style and personality all of its own,
www.peepshow.org.uk.

It's a two-way street
The way relationships work in the creative
industry is exactly the same as the way they
work outside it. There's a healthy element of
'you scratch my back and I'll scratch yours',
which keeps the wheels rolling. As you go
about building and maintaining relationships
throughout the industry (and outside of it),
opportunities will come your way. The nature
of operating as an individual freelance creative
dictates that you can't accept every work
assignment you are offered. On some
occasions your workload may simply be too
heavy; on others the project under discussion
may be outside of your scope. These are both
excellent opportunities to add some benefit to
your network of contacts. For example, if a
prospective client mentions some illustration
work – and you are, say, a copywriter – it's

GETTING YOUR DIGITAL PORTFOLIO OVER TO A PROSPECTIVE
CLIENT LAYS THE FOUNDATIONS FOR FUTURE WORK BECAUSE
YOU LEAVE IT WITH THEM.

always a good idea to recommend some outstanding illustrators. If the client uses one of your contacts, that's work for your illustrator and a favour for the client. Think about the ways in which digital media can streamline this: regular emails with links to work opportunities you have heard about; a website that details your latest projects and potential opportunities for other creatives.

There are plenty of other ways in which you can add value to your network. Introducing associates with potentially mutually beneficial talents and interests, for example. Think about the various roles you can play within your network and explore ways in which you can add value. Again, digital channels can play a key role in this. Not only is it the ideal medium for keeping your network connected – it also provides a platform for you and your network to bring things to life. The Peepshow collective is a perfect example: a group of talented friends who used a website to display their work, whilst opening it up to the widest audience. Digital gives you a forum in which you can keep a close network of friends and colleagues in touch or a platform for creating something that evolves into a living, breathing brand.

EMAILING DIGITAL SAMPLES OF YOUR WORK IS A GREAT INTRODUCTION.

onelouder ▶▶

31 yurong street
east sydney nsw 2010
call +61 2 9380 9011
fax +61 2 9380 9866
www.onelouder.com.au
email hq@onelouder.com.au

31 yurong street
east sydney nsw 2010
call +61 2 9380 9011
fax +61 2 9380 9866

onelou

31 yurong street
east sydney nsw 2010
call +61 2 9380 9011
fax +61 2 9380 9866

onelou

withcomps/cd/**sticker**/video/**going**to

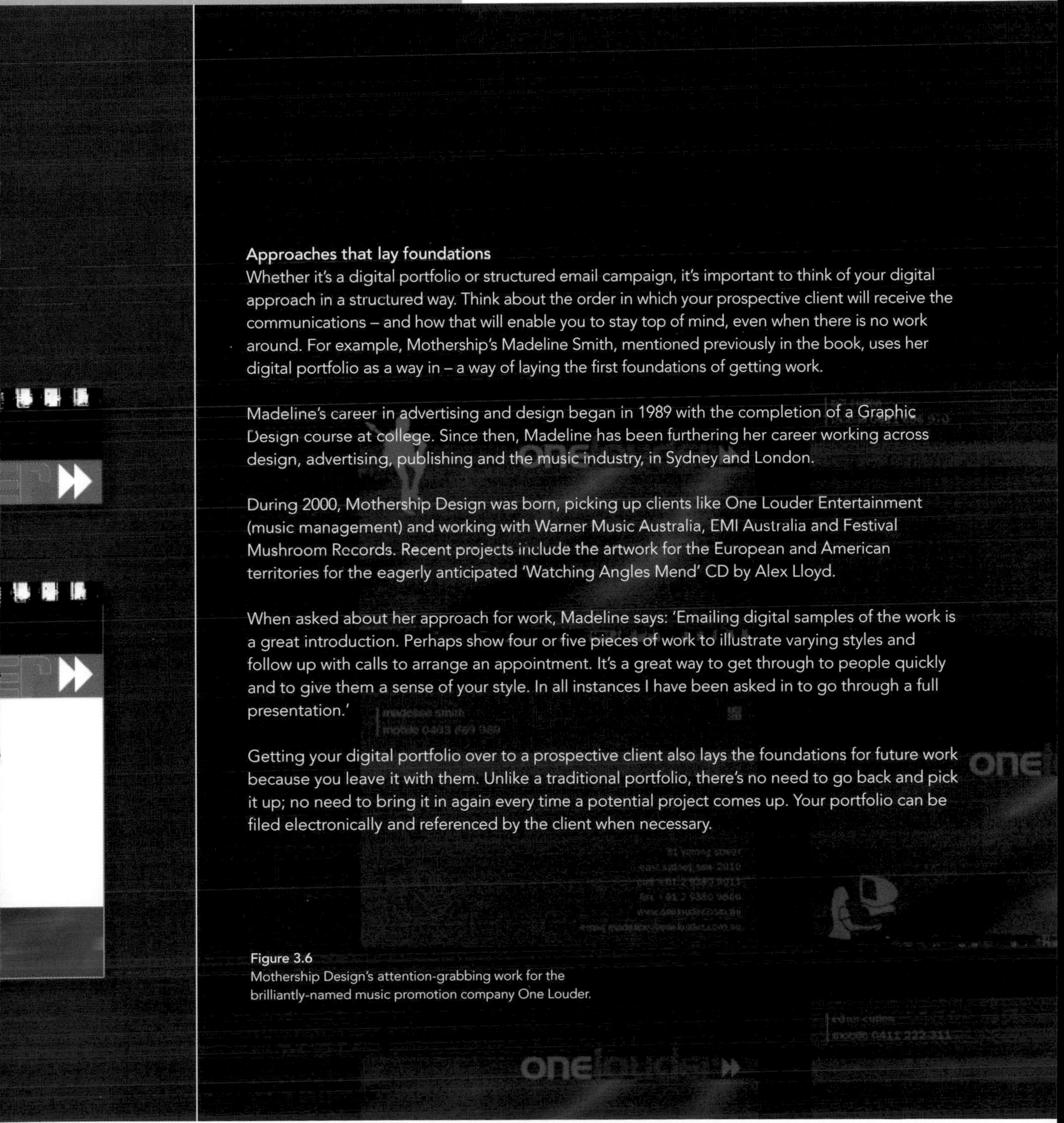

Approaches that lay foundations

Whether it's a digital portfolio or structured email campaign, it's important to think of your digital approach in a structured way. Think about the order in which your prospective client will receive the communications – and how that will enable you to stay top of mind, even when there is no work around. For example, Mothership's Madeline Smith, mentioned previously in the book, uses her digital portfolio as a way in – a way of laying the first foundations of getting work.

Madeline's career in advertising and design began in 1989 with the completion of a Graphic Design course at college. Since then, Madeline has been furthering her career working across design, advertising, publishing and the music industry, in Sydney and London.

During 2000, Mothership Design was born, picking up clients like One Louder Entertainment (music management) and working with Warner Music Australia, EMI Australia and Festival Mushroom Records. Recent projects include the artwork for the European and American territories for the eagerly anticipated 'Watching Angles Mend' CD by Alex Lloyd.

When asked about her approach for work, Madeline says: 'Emailing digital samples of the work is a great introduction. Perhaps show four or five pieces of work to illustrate varying styles and follow up with calls to arrange an appointment. It's a great way to get through to people quickly and to give them a sense of your style. In all instances I have been asked in to go through a full presentation.'

Getting your digital portfolio over to a prospective client also lays the foundations for future work because you leave it with them. Unlike a traditional portfolio, there's no need to go back and pick it up; no need to bring it in again every time a potential project comes up. Your portfolio can be filed electronically and referenced by the client when necessary.

Figure 3.6
Mothership Design's attention-grabbing work for the
brilliantly-named music promotion company One Louder.

Figure 3.7
The West London-based Grand Union is an expert at using
digital media to bring brands and customers together,
www.thegrandunion.com.

TIP – *When emailing prospective clients examples of work, three or
four pieces are usually enough to get an interview.*

Email and e-zines

These are two great ways of using new technology to your advantage. To start with, email takes
away the need for the traditional round of phone call after phone call. It enables you to
demonstrate a keenness and passion for a subject and a thorough understanding of how the
digital medium can be effectively used for communication purposes. It can be used in a number
of ways, from the quick note to keep in touch with existing clients, to the full HTML email to
market you to new clients. The medium is a way of developing and building a relationship with a
potential employer whilst having the potential to impress by providing ready-made insights into
digital marketing: you never know when your thoughts and ideas may get used in other people's
client status meetings, perhaps leading to a project.

At the other end of the email spectrum is the 'e-zine'. This is a catch-all term to describe a large
number of executions. When used effectively, it can build your brand, grow your client list and
keep clients coming to you for a range of services. A great example is the monthly Global
Content Review (GCR) produced by Grand Union – a London-based communications agency that
focuses on digital channels as a means to bring brands and customers together.

Figure 3.8
Grand Union's Global Content Review (GCR) inspires
debate and strengthens the company's brand and
steadily increases its network of contacts.

THE GCR IS NOT A HARD SELLING TOOL, BUT HELPS GET GRAND
UNION UNDER THE CLIENT RADAR AND HOPEFULLY FRONT OF MIND.

Grand Union was launched by people with
diverse blue chip backgrounds in advertising,
publishing, gaming and business consultancy.
The philosophy of the agency delivers
marketing solutions in a range of digital
channels, from online (websites, rich media,
streaming media) to mobile (SMS, MMS),
gaming and iTV. However, as the boundaries
between digital and non-digital channels
continue to blur, the agency is working to
deliver full creative solutions.

Grand Union's GCR email newsletter goes
out monthly to people that sign up to the
newsletter on thegrandunion.com site,
including clients and interested parties in the
marketing industry. It takes a particular subject
or issue and demonstrates how it is being
discussed, explored, challenged and brought
to life through digital channels. The subject
areas are as diverse as music, viral marketing,
gaming and how kids use text messaging.

However, the focus of the GCR is getting an
understanding of how digital channels are
affecting marketing and the wider world. The
GCR adds value on a number of levels. Firstly,
it is a way of keeping Grand Union in touch
with its contacts and friends in the industry.
Secondly, it ensures Grand Union is kept up to
speed with what's new in the digital arena.
Thirdly, it aims to be interesting and useful
enough to be spread virally, potentially
generating new business opportunities for
Grand Union. Rob Forshaw a founding partner
of the agency says that the GCR 'is not a hard
selling tool but helps get Grand Union under
the client radar and hopefully front of mind.'

ROB FORSHAW, GRAND UNION

Grand Union's Global Content Review is one way of building up a network of contacts, but it's not difficult to do something similar on a smaller level. For example, you could build something around your areas of interest. Whether that's snowboarding, music or sea fishing, you could turn a hobby into something of interest and use to a network of others. This could be done by building a website devoted to your hobby or producing a regular email report on the topic. You could turn this into a GCR-style e-zine bulletin by getting friends who share your interest to contribute articles to the piece. By making it a regularly updated and mailed out digital piece, it will add value to your network and keep people interested.

Figure 3.9
The Major Players recruitment agency website,
www.majorplayers.co.uk.

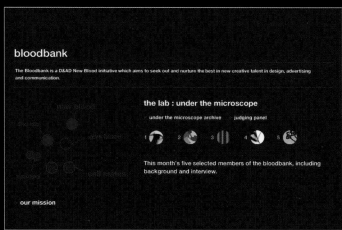

Figure 3.10
The D&AD bloodbank young creative talent website,
www.dandad.co.uk.

Figure 3.11
Australia's Young Guns website, www.ygaward.com.

Pooling your talents

Collaboration is an excellent way for freelance creatives to go about getting work. There are two main ways in which you can do this:

1. Pooling your talents with colleagues from the same field as you.
2. Pooling your talents with colleagues from different, but related fields.

The former is an excellent way of offering clients a wide choice of styles within a specific area. As we mentioned in Section One, the illustrators' collective, Peepshow (www.peepshow.org.uk) is an excellent example. Combining traditional illustrators' talents with state-of-the-art Web design, the site is an interactive gallery of outstanding illustration work. The site displays a breadth of styles probably not achievable by an individual illustrator. It also acts as a forum for excellent illustration work, a focus point for other illustrators and the wider creative industry.

Alternatively, collaborating with creatives from separate, related fields enables you to offer clients a wider service, while maintaining a flexible freelance approach. A small collective of designers and writers can act as a 'mini agency' servicing clients by sharing work among the collective. It's a set-up that enables everyone to stay freelance, while increasing the chances of getting work from a wider range of clients than you could as an individual freelance resource.

Recruitment agencies like Major Players, London (www.majorplayers.co.uk) can put you in touch with other creatives looking to team up, or you can find contacts through organisations such as the D&AD (www.dandad.co.uk) and Young Guns (www.ygaward.com) in Australia.

Figure 3.12
Stills from Venla Kivilahti's funky website www.venla.net
(above and previous spread).

How digital media can facilitate collaboration

Digital channels can enable you to get work as a collective. You could use an intranet to collaborate with friends anywhere in the world on projects. Intranets enable the team to work on various parts of a project – a website, for example – simultaneously. A website is an excellent way to set up a collaboration and to market a diverse range of skills. The team could comprise designers, writers, illustrators, photographers, and programmers. By each member of the website team spreading the word in their respective field, the website can quickly become well known.

The more technically advanced you are the better: taking the principle one step further, you could set up an extranet to market the collective's skills to potential clients. These are good ways of marketing joint skills – while keeping you in touch with your network.

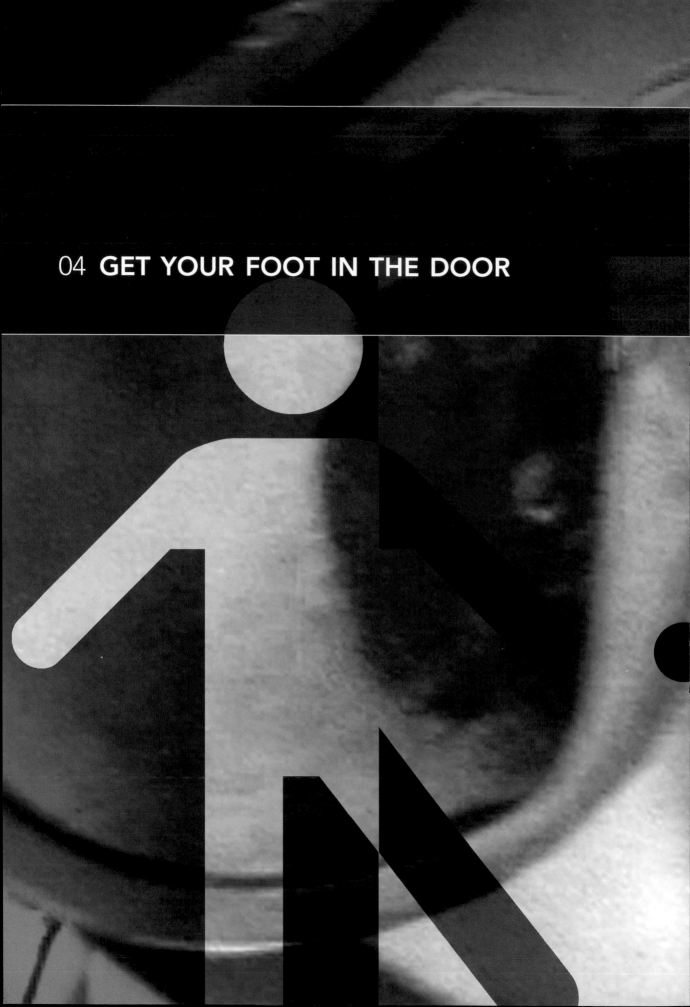

04 **GET YOUR FOOT IN THE DOOR**

Think strategically about how to market yourself

It's a simple fact of the marketing industry that the best creative solutions are built around a business need. The creative solutions that work the hardest by cutting through and communicating with their intended audience are those that take as their starting point a business need, requirement or problem. Rooting the creative work in that requirement means that on some level it addresses the problem, it attempts to offer a solution – ultimately it answers the brief.

This problem-solving approach to creativity is evident in all of the best work, from Avis's 'We're No. 2, so we try harder' ads to the Orange 'the future's bright…' campaign. You'll find it everywhere today, from VW's brilliantly lateral television ads to Apple Mac's powerful branding work and BMW's famous Internet film series. These are examples of strong work produced by strong creatives for strong clients. They're creative solutions that answer real consumer needs: for affordable, reliable cars, for new technology that enhances their lives, for entertainment.

So, your clients are being asked for strategically clever, integrated solutions. To get work, you need to show in your approach that you can think and work in this way. Digital channels provide great opportunities to do exactly that; they are an excellent way to reach potential clients – quickly, cleverly, relevantly. However, our research for this book has shown that the potential of digital approaches is not yet being exploited fully throughout the industry. Interesting, intelligent approaches such as Madeline Smith's digital 'book' and the Peepshow collective's illustration website are not thus far the norm, which is yet another reason for you to consider a digital approach.

Figure 4.0
Poster design for a Nike product, the Nike Infinity.
Produced on sticker paper with over 60 different swooshes, fans are able to remove the stickers and try them on their shoes.
Artist: Cyprien Gaillard. Design: Kasia Korczak.
Copywriter: Payam Sharifi.

Figure 4.1
Screengrabs from Alastair Green's USBX collective snowboarding website, www.usbx.co.uk.

TIP – *As you start thinking about strategic ways of marketing yourself, speak to strategists, planners, account people and clients.*

As you start thinking about strategic ways of marketing yourself, speak to people. To strategists, planners, account people and clients. And, as we discussed earlier in the book, explore ways of creating and developing your own brand as a demonstration of your abilities. Bring your life, your hobbies and interests together creatively. Whatever you're into – from skateboarding to sushi, deep sea fishing to deep house music – use digital media to wrap it all together, then take it to a client and sell it. Alastair Green's snowboarding website is an excellent example of this. 'A new media creative who snowboards – isn't that a shock,' he jokes. However, by combining his passion for new media with his passion for snowboarding, he's created an outstanding showcase for his talents. The site is a living, breathing forum for new design work and a great focal point for his snowboarding posse. Of this kind of personal brand-building, Tim Heyward says: 'The ability to create individual stardom and market their brand is much more innate in young people today. Platforms such as DJing and the dotcom phenomenon showed that ordinary punters can create a brand and make themselves or their product famous.'

Figure 4.2
Included in Mother's promotional book are executions
from their award-winning campaign for Britart.com.

EVERYTHING OUT THERE HAS ALREADY BEEN DONE — THE SUCCESS WILL COME FROM CREATING AND IMPLEMENTING NEW WAYS OF THINKING AND WORKING.

New ways of thinking about old problems

As ever with any creative endeavour, the currency is in the new. Everything out there has already been done – the success will come from creating and implementing new ways of thinking and working. Think again about BMW's decision to market their cars through an Internet-only campaign. It's a bold move that shows courage and vision. How can you bring new thinking to the table for your clients? How can you help them break through boundaries of marketing overkill and consumer indifference?

On the subject of cutting through indifference, Tim Heyward says: 'Not only have "ordinary" people become ad literate and cynical but the barriers to entry for delivering marketing communications have evaporated. Technology is no longer an inhibitor and whilst "old school" advertisers are struggling to understand its place, young kids and smart agencies are exploiting it.'

“ ”

BMW found a cut-through solution to the challenge of reaching a jaded audience – with the Internet. Where will the new solutions come from? And can you lead the way? If the answer's 'yes'; if you can deliver fresh thinking on traditional marketing problems – 'how can I communicate with a consumer who's not interested in what I have to say?'; 'how can I sell my service to a consumer who's convinced that a competitive service is better?'; 'why should I advertise in magazines when research shows my target market doesn't read them anymore?' – you need to find a way to demonstrate it. It's no longer enough to be talented – in today's crowded creative marketplace, you need to find a way to market that talent. Think about how digital channels can facilitate the process.

I LIKE TO SEE PEOPLE WHO ARE THINKING DIFFERENTLY AND DEMONSTRATING CREATIVITY IN DIFFERENT MEDIA — TAXIS AND WEBSITES, FOR EXAMPLE.

Figure 4.3
The power of having a unique personality:
everything Mother does has a very distinct voice,
www.motherlondon.com.

Avoiding pigeonholes

With the evolution of the creative industries away from exclusive specialists and towards widely skilled, diversely talented creatives, broadening your horizons is obviously a good idea. Being pigeonholed can be potentially disastrous for the freelance creative: the moment your particular area of expertise goes quiet can be the moment your source of work dries up.

Mark Whelan at Cake says: 'Don't think about content. Think about the routes to that content.' It's a way of communicating the fact that, as the sixties thinker Marshall MacLuhan once famously said, 'the medium is the message'. Ideas, although they are the lifeblood of any creative endeavour, are only half the story. Without ways of presenting and delivering those ideas effectively, they become irrelevant.

MARK WAITES, MOTHER

“ ”

TIP – *Always be looking a year down the track for new industry trends, new opportunities, new ways to implement your talents and the skills you are constantly learning.*

The call for creative diversity is clear at Cake. 'We have a group of people who excel in creative ways and who are professionals in different disciplines,' says Mark Whelan. Mother also places an emphasis on widescreen thinking. 'We look for disciplined, responsible creatives who can work all aspects of the business – media, strategy, project management,' says Mark Waites. He continues: 'If you are a creative embracing new ways of communicating, this should be reflected in the work. I like to see people who are thinking differently and demonstrating it in different media – taxis and websites, for example.' Again, the key is thinking outside of traditional boundaries – in terms of creative, media and strategy. As Mark Waites says: 'Great media is always creatively led – the best creatives are the best strategic thinkers.'

Figure 4.4
Mother's tongue-in-cheek promotional 'Punch Tastic'
gold sovereign, www.motherlondon.com.

Try to avoid the natural pitfalls. If you're a packaging designer, speak to people about design, print, posters, and the Web. If you're an illustrator, look to diversify in terms of style – or look to branch out from print to the Web. It's easy for photographers to get pigeonholed: as a still life specialist, a portrait photographer, or a car photographer. Branch out. Think about new styles. Ask for advice. Consider training of some kind. Look into new ways of working. The same goes for writers, art directors, and Web designers. Whatever your creative field, always be looking for ways to expand the boundaries, to work in new areas, in new styles, with new people – and ways digital channels can help. Remember, if what you're doing doesn't scare you, you're operating in your comfort zone and that's never a good sign for creative people.

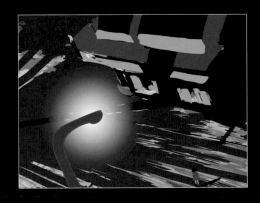

Figure 4.5
'Tangerine's Dream' – an interactive animation by Venla Kivilahti about a woman drawn into a strange world of paintings.

BEING PIGEONHOLED CAN BE POTENTIALLY DISASTROUS FOR
THE FREELANCE CREATIVE.

Figure 4.6
Venla Kivilahti's 'Phantasmal Voyage' interactive digital video (background image) is a metaphor for life being a journey across a dark bridge.

Building a varied portfolio

The end product of a move towards creative diversity is a varied portfolio. Your portfolio is your key to work; one that shows examples of work on varied projects is a passport to further commissions on a wide range of products. Try to structure your portfolio so that it articulates your talents in an intelligent way; organise it in an order that makes logical sense and gives you an almost narrative storyline to talk through when you present the portfolio in person.

Venla Kivilahti, the interactive designer of the 'Feeling for all the People' animated film discussed earlier in the book, understands that a diverse portfolio is the key to work. 'While my portfolio consists mainly of recent multimedia pieces, I understand that I have to show diversity by building new elements into it. I need to add more traditional design pieces to balance it out. That's why I want to keep building my portfolio over the next few years.'

Alastair Green is constantly looking for new ways of turning personal projects into a showcase for his skills. He says: 'I tend to play with a lot of new media in my spare time. It has always been a habit; from fun screensavers to home-made DVDs and so on. It's just an extension of that, by finishing them and then including them as personal projects for my portfolio.'

TIP – Structure your portfolio in an order that makes logical sense and gives you a narrative storyline to talk through when you present it in person.

Mothership Design's Madeline Smith
recognises the importance of a varied
portfolio. 'My portfolio is my key point of
contact with prospective clients,' she says. 'I
have worked for a wide range of clients, in a
number of different media. I have also applied
my skills across many areas of advertising and
design. The presentation needs to
demonstrate that diversity, while showcasing
the cream of my work. It's really a well-
organised, well-presented "best of" package.'

Now happily employed in the advertising
industry on a permanent basis, Madeline uses
Mothership Design as a freelance outlet for her
wider creative skills. 'Mothership enables me
to explore my creativity outside of advertising.
I use it as an outlet for my wider interests in
design and creating brands. Whether it be for
huge corporate clients or alternative music
artists, the process of starting with a base
"product" and sculpting it into something that
people want to buy into on an emotional level,
is a very exciting process.'

Mothership Design is an excellent example of
the way in which many freelance-to-permanent
creatives keep their talents fresh. It's a way of
structuring your work/interest balance, of
exploring ideas outside of the briefs you work
on every day and of building variety into your
portfolio.

Figure 4.7
Print to screen: a Venla Kivilahti project which
involved transferring Frank Miller's Sin City comics
into a digital format.

Be on the look out for opportunities

Once you're at the point that every freelance creative aims for: a varied client list, regular work, and a growing, evolving portfolio of work you're proud of, it would be tempting to relax, to sit back and expect the work to keep flowing in. In fact, this is the key moment in the career of every freelance creative. It's the period of time when you need to be using success to breed success; meeting new contacts through existing ones, seeing potential new clients and considering collaborations. Digital media provides a number of ways of doing this, from email newsletters to regularly updated websites.

While there are many upsides to being busy, the downside is that it's easy to take your eye off the ball. Freelance work is traditionally 'feast or famine' – manically busy or spookily quiet – so it's essential to keep your eyes open for new contacts, openings and opportunities. Being proactive is a key skill here. Mark Whelan of Cake, for example, values 'professionals who are good at what they do and get on and do it.'

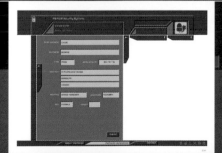

Figure 4.8
Chloe George's Memicon Security System website is
a pictorial 'memory code' designed to replace
conventional PIN codes, www.chloegeorge.co.uk.

ALWAYS MAKE THINGS AS SIMPLE AND ACCESSIBLE AS POSSIBLE FOR PROSPECTIVE CLIENTS.

Figure 4.9
Chloe George created a website that gives the
Brownies a contemporary feel, www.chloegeorge.co.uk.

Keep your antenna set to 'on' in the search for work: in the freelance game, proactivity is as important as talent. Another proactive young creative is Chloe George. A talented designer who won a D&AD pencil for Website Design in the student section, Chloe created the Memicon Security System for a competitive brief. In her own words, the system is 'a highly individual, pictorial, sequential – memory code. It's designed to replace the traditional forms of security such as PIN codes. The aim is to ensure that the images are etched on the user's memory. The Memicon Security System, available on- and offline, allows the user to assign an appropriate icon to six significant memories from his or her past. These icons are put into chronological order, which then becomes a highly individual, pictorial, sequential, memory code, which is used by the creator as his or her multipurpose security code or Memicon. By using images to associate personal memories in the user's life, it makes it much easier to remember.' The project was an excellent showcase for Chloe's interactive design and programming skills. It led to work as a 'designer/animator/account manager' with Random Media, London.

TIP – *Take your talent, personality, contacts, background and experience, and think about ways you can use digital channels to turn them into a reason to hire you.*

Remember, every project is an opportunity to build new relationships. Whether it's a work placement, a first job or a freelance project, use every commission to speak to people, to seek out new work, to get phone numbers, email addresses, and chances to get your portfolio in front of new people. Whenever you're busy, take a minute to think ahead into the future. What will your next freelance project be? The one after that? And the one after that? Think about how digital channels can help you get ahead. Can you do some work on your client's own website? Does the website have an area where you can display your work? Is someone you're working with involved in a Web project that could be a further outlet for your work? Keep exploring the digital possibilities.

Turning negatives into positives

This section is all about getting your foot in the door. It's the most important thing for any freelance creative. Once in, you have an opportunity, a chance to demonstrate your talents. But up to that moment, you are on the outside looking in. So what do we mean by 'turning negatives into positives'? We mean use everything you can to your advantage. Take everything – your talent, your personality, your contacts, your background, your experience – and think about ways you can use digital channels to turn them into a reason to hire you for a project. Perhaps we should have called this section 'accentuate the positives'; or, even better, 'eliminate the negatives'.

A point to remember is to always make things as simple and accessible as possible for prospective clients. 'Just show some parts of the work – not everything. Three or four pieces of work are enough to get an interview,' says Alastair Green. Consider your approach. Are you sending in your CV? Which format would be most accessible for your prospective client? Are you posting a CD-ROM? Will it work on Mac and PC? And will the client have time to go through it? And if they do, is the content laid out in an organised way? Think about the approach carefully – it's the thing that's going to get you through the client's door. Whether you are sending a digital portfolio or making a phone call, emailing a creative director or leaving your portfolio with the PA, think about ways to enhance your chances. Tailor the approach for the recipient; make sure there are no technical problems with your piece; avoid spelling mistakes and typos on letters and CVs like the plague.

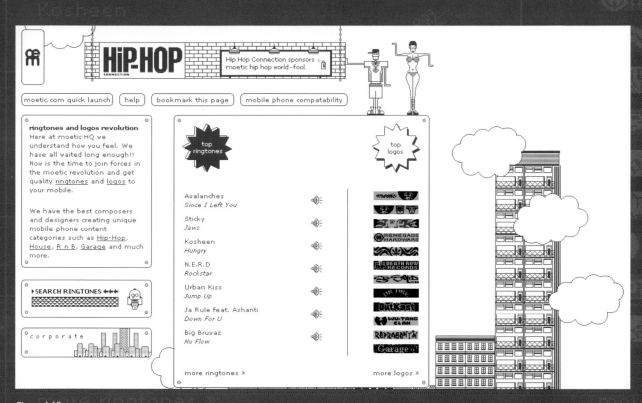

Figure 4.10
Moetic's ringtones website, www.moetic.com.

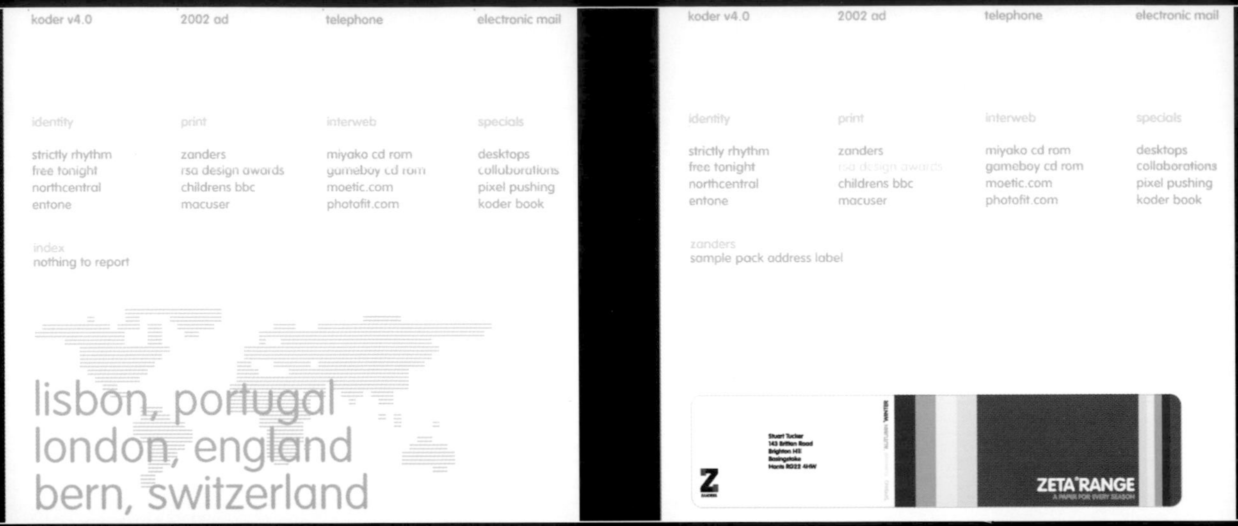

Figure 4.11
Design aesthetics: the Koder website.

ANY DESIGNER CAN BE TAUGHT HOW TO USE A COMPUTER AND DESIGN WEBSITES, BUT GOOD IDEAS ARE FEW AND FAR BETWEEN.

The medium isn't the idea

Whether you're an advertising creative, a Web designer or a photographer, your work will come from a core idea. Ideas are currency – that's the nature of creativity. So while it's important to think outside traditional media boundaries, to explore new ways of working and new ways of executing and delivering creative ideas, it's important to remember that without an idea in the first place, you don't have anything to deliver.

Alastair Green comments: 'the things that will impress a potential employer are enthusiasm, a passion for the work and evidence of good ideas. Any designer can be taught how to use a computer and design websites, but good ideas – they are few and far between.'

| koder v4.0 | 2002 ad | telephone | electronic mail |

identity	print	interweb	specials
strictly rhythm	zanders	miyako cd rom	desktops
free tonight	rsa design awards	gameboy cd rom	collaborations
northcentral	childrens bbc	moetic.com	pixel pushing
entone	macuser	photofit.com	koder book

childrens bbc

(front)

ALASTAIR GREEN, OGILVY INTERACTIVE   " "

So, new creative channels are important. Yes, you need to think outside of press ads, packaging, banner ads, whatever the dominant medium of the day may be. But you always need to start with an idea. While Mark Whelan is prescient in his advice that 'media is where the power lies' and his call to 'think about the routes to content', he doesn't mean abandon ideas. He means think about new ways to get to them, to come up with them, to execute them, to demonstrate them effectively. He's talking about new, supremely relevant, highly targeted ways for creative people to communicate ideas with the audience they have been created for.

A-D

Christmas/Noël01

Figure 4.12
A very 'Mother' Christmas: Mother often subverts conventional formats to deliver its message, www.motherlondon.com.

TIP – *You can dress up as Superman and stand outside an agency all day to get noticed, but that's not rooted in a relevant idea. It doesn't actually demonstrate an understanding of a creative problem.*

This kind of thinking needs to be evident in everything from your approach to getting work, to the work itself. As Mark Waites from Mother says, you can dress up as Superman and stand outside the agency all day to get noticed, but that's not rooted in a relevant idea. It doesn't actually demonstrate an understanding of a creative problem.

Tim Heyward agrees. He also has some interesting thoughts on the trend for agencies to develop bland ideas, designed to work in a number of internal markets: 'Internationalism is a huge factor in contemporary advertising. FMCG and car companies are increasingly creating advertising vehicles that work in any country, using Eastern European faces that could be from anywhere. The storyline is bland enough to suit any national psyche and the voice-overs are easily dubbed into the appropriate language.'

Whether you think that's a good or bad thing, its effect on the way the creative industry works is far-reaching. The producer-based model is becoming more popular – and that's arguably a good thing for freelance creatives. Don't just target creative directors; get in touch with producers too. But, most of all, when you're thinking about how to market your creativity, think about ideas. When you're considering and crafting your approach to get work, try to demonstrate an understanding and appreciation of ideas. An idea is essential when you're working on a brief – and that's exactly what you're doing: working on the brief of getting yourself hired.

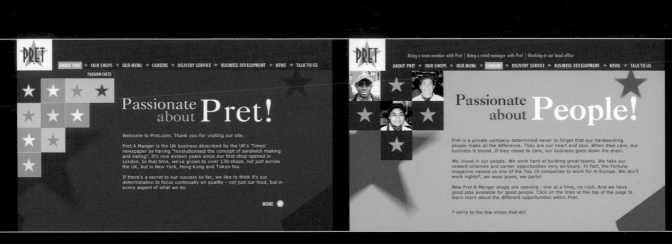

Figure 4.13
Simplicity is a powerful weapon: Pret A Manger's website, www.pret.com.

TIP – *The best way to cut through remains simplicity of thought.*

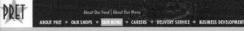

Keep it simple, stupid

When asked what he thinks employers are looking for, Alastair Green is straight to the point: 'Simple ideas done well.' While the importance of the idea cannot be overstated, the key to its success is in keeping it simple. 'Keep it simple, stupid' is an old advertising dictum that has lost none of its relevance today. In an age of special effects, digital design options and a breathtaking variety of ways to execute creative solutions, the best way to cut through, remains what Maurice and Charles Saatchi call 'brutal simplicity of thought'.

It's there to see in the intelligence of the VW ads, the purity of Pret A Manger packaging and the smart simplicity of Ikea as a brand. It's there in every Nike brand communication you see, in every New Order record or CD cover, everything Orange does as a brand and every Penguin book cover.

Use this way of thinking and working when you're putting together your portfolio, planning your approach to get work and actually working. Whether you're a website designer, a photographer or an art director, the principle is the same. Sit down and think before you turn on the computer. Alastair Green says: 'When I got my first job, my art director told me that my portfolio, which I designed and built in Director, was the first one that he had received that worked. The reason why? Because I kept it simple.'

Remember this as you work within digital channels to market your creativity. Keep things simple and stay focused on ideas. It's what your job is about – and why it's a privilege to work as a creative.

Putting it all into practice

Now for the important part: getting out there and getting the work. It's time to put the book down and put your plan into action. Whether you're new to the industry, still finding your feet or you're an experienced freelance creative, think about ways that digital media can give you an edge. Consider everything from an email campaign to a digital portfolio to a website and beyond. There's a wide range of ways in which new technology can help you get work. But before you start the process of approaching creative directors, producers and other potential clients, think carefully about the creative industry and your place in it.

As we said at the start of the book, these are times of change. Success for you will be dependent on gauging the mood of these times – and the way people work within them. For example, highly organised, diversely talented creatives are in demand. Creatives who aren't afraid of deadlines, new ways of working and new media channels. Do you have these attributes? And, crucially, do you demonstrate them in your approach to getting work?

One way that you can add a positive angle to your approach is by being proactive from the start. Get smart about the way you get contacts. Be open to opportunities. And be ready to take those opportunities when they come your way. Digital channels are excellent facilitators for the process. And, in addition to getting your message out to potential clients, think about ways in which you can bring them to you. Whether you're starting an email newsletter to build up a network of contacts, running your own regularly-updated website or showcasing some animation work you've done on a friend's website, look for ways to demonstrate your talent.

It's all part of the essential process described in Chapter Two: building the 'brand of you'. Remember, this is the most important brand you will work on in your entire career. Everything you do will impact on it. So whether you're planning your approach to getting work or actually working for a client, keep that impact in mind – and use it as an inspiration.

As some of the interviewees in this book have stated, you should use every avenue open to you to develop the 'brand of you'. Use every ounce of your talent to get your message out there. Whether that means running a club, DJing, starting a magazine or building a website, channel your creativity into ideas – both inside and outside of the industry you work in. Creative inspiration might come from an item on the news, the fabric of a man's jumper on the tube, an article in the paper or something a lady in the supermarket says to you. Get out into the world and soak up all the culture and ideas. Then use digital channels to demonstrate your unique perspective and sell it to creative directors.

While your perspective as a creative person is your most marketable asset, remember the importance of the way you market it. While digital media enables you to get your message to prospective clients clearly, think about the way you use it. Don't over-complicate things. Too much technology is not necessarily a good thing. Whether it's a website link, a CD-ROM or an online portfolio, make sure the technology works, runs smoothly and doesn't take forever to download. A beautifully designed and executed piece of digital direct mail is useless if the person you've sent it to gets bored waiting for something to happen and goes off to do something else instead.

Timing is key. Just as a piece of digital direct mail that takes too long to download can mean a missed opportunity, so can a piece sent at the wrong time. Get in touch with a prospective client on the wrong day or in the wrong month and it could be a wasted opportunity. So make sure you do as much research as possible. Is the agency you're approaching looking for new creative resource? Is it their traditional quiet period? Is the person you're contacting likely to have time to look at your portfolio? Are they too busy? Are they on holiday? Are they still the right person to contact? These are all things to consider before you get in touch.

Don't ever forget the importance of building and maintaining relationships. Start early – at school, college, and your first job – and keep working at it. Build different networks. And look for ways digital channels can keep you in touch with those networks – from running a website based around a joint interest like www.usbx.co.uk, sending out an email bulletin that adds value through links and information, like Chinwag, or collaborating on joint projects with friends around the world, using intranets and extranets.

But while we're enthusiastic about digital media, please don't think that the message of this book is that the idea must take a back seat to technology in today's creative industry. That isn't the case. Digital channels are important to creative people – as facilitators and as ways of expressing creativity. Ways of getting highly relevant messages to highly targeted audiences. You don't need to become a 'techie' – or even know much about technology. It's a simple case of understanding as much as you need to in order to exploit its opportunities.

The key thing is to keep honing your skills and developing new skills. Keep looking for new ways of working and new people to work with. However you market yourself and your creativity, strive for simplicity. Just as when you're working on a brief for a client, one message per communication remains the golden rule. One message that, if expressed and executed correctly, can make an impact on your potential client.

Stay focused on the unique skills you can offer your clients. On the ways you can grow this offering. Because, as you build your interests, relationships and ideas – your life – into your work, you will become more marketable as a creative resource.

'KEEP IT SIMPLE, STUPID' IS AN OLD ADVERTISING DICTUM WHICH HAS LOST NONE OF ITS RELEVANCE TODAY.

""

www.dandad.co.uk
British Design & Art Direction's website.

www.majorplayers.co.uk
London-based creative recruitment agency.

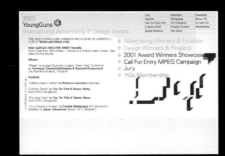

www.eatmail.tv
Access the latest guerrilla advertising campaigns.

www.cakemedia.com
The Cake Group website.

www.folkdevil.com
An ever-changing online forum of esoteric debate.

www.thegrandunion.com
The Grand Union website.

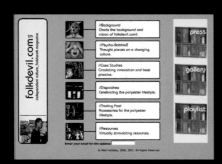

www.ygaward.com
The Young Guns creative awards website.

www.peepshow.org.uk
The cutting edge illustration website.

www.usbx.co.uk
The website of Alastair Green's snowboarding collective.

www.gorillaz.com
The famous Gorillaz website.

www.motherlondon.com
The Mother website.

Books

The New Marketing Manifesto:
Successful Brands in the 21st Century
by John Grant
(Texere Publishing)

After Image:
Mind-expanding Marketing
by John Grant
(Profile Business)

Welcome to the Creative Age:
Bananas, Business and the Death of Marketing
by Mark Earls
(John Wiley & Sons)

Brand New Thinking:
Brought to Life by 11 Experts Who Do
edited by Merry Baskin and
Mark Earls
(Kogan Page)

Disruption:
Overwhelming Conventions and
Shaking Up the Marketplace
by Jean-Marie Dru
(An Adweek Book)

Acknowledgements
We would like to thank Natalia Price-Cabrera, Editorial Director at AVA Publishing, for her enthusiasm and guidance. Thanks too must go to Mark Waites, Mark Whelan, Tom Thorne, Fred Flade, Dan Douglas, Tim Heyward, Toby Bradbury, Alastair Green, Venla Kivilahti, Chloe George, Philip Kitching, Tom Northey, Lucy McLauchlan, Matt Watkins, James-Lee Duffy, Dominic Franks, Kasia Korczak, Madeline Smith, Rob Forshaw, Isaac Wong, Sam Michel, Caroline Perry, Benji Wiedemann and Lisa Ha. Their encouragement and involvement in the project is greatly appreciated. Finally we would like to thank Mark Roberts for his design work on this book.